The New HARDCORE BODYBUILDING

The New HARDCORE BODYBUILDING

ROBERT KENNEDY

Sterling Publishing Co., Inc. New York

Library of Congress Cataloging-in-Publication Data

Kennedy, Robert, 1938–
The new hardcore bodybuilding / Robert Kennedy.
p. cm.
Rev. ed. of: Hardcore bodybuilding. 1982.
Includes index.
1. Bodybuilding. I. Kennedy, Robert, 1938– Hardcore bodybuilding. II. Title. III. Title: New hard core body building. IV. Title: New hard core bodybuilding.
GV546.5.K45 1990
646.7'5—dc20 90-39881
CIP

10 9 8

Published by Sterling Publishing Company, Inc.
387 Park Avenue South, New York, N.Y. 10016
Based on *Hardcore Bodybuilding* © 1982 by Robert Kennedy
Distributed in Canada by Sterling Publishing
℅ Canadian Manda Group, P.O. Box 920, Station U
Toronto, Ontario, Canada M8Z 5P9
Distributed in Great Britain and Europe by Cassell PLC
Villiers House, 41/47 Strand, London WC2N 5JE, England
Distributed in Australia by Capricorn Ltd.
P.O. Box 665, Lane Cove, NSW 2066
Manufactured in the United States of America

Sterling ISBN 0-8069-7480-X

CONTENTS

Chris Dickerson at 50, posing at the Arnold Classic, Columbus, Ohio.

Your chest is feeling thicker, larger. The pecs are heavier . . . the pump is not far away. You sit on the end of the exercise bench, and as you roll your body backwards to lie face up, your head barely misses the loaded barbell. You have done it a thousand times before: the surroundings, the bench, the bar are familiar.

You stare up at the heavy iron little more than a foot above your face, shuffle your feet and jiggle your "glutes" so that your entire body is balanced solidly, ready to launch the bar into space. Both hands grab the knurling, leaving equal distance from either collar. You check visually and move one hand out a tenth of an inch. HUPP! The bar rises, bearing down hard against the thumbless palms of your hands. To the uninitiated it appears precariously balanced, but you know better. You gulp air and

FOREWORD

your waist vanishes into your chest, now swelling and surging with newly summoned strength. The bar lowers slowly to your sternum, kissing the pecs with light precision, which in turn signals the triceps and pectorals to propel the weight upwards. As they straighten, you explode air from your lungs like a noisy piston and once again throw your muscles into reverse. The bar lowers to the sternum. Smoothly, cautiously, the weight rises . . . falls . . . rises. Only at the tenth repetition do invigoration and confidence yield to stress and anxiety. You counter by mentally reasserting your aggressiveness. A curse forms on your lips. The bar *has* to go up two more times. Sweat stings your eyes. You blink repeatedly to focus on the shaking bar at the end of your extended arms. Momentarily you question attempting the pain-

Dave Draper keeps an eye on Arnold Schwarzenegger during the press-behind-neck.

ful madness of two more reps. Your muscles read your mind's doubt and the bar feels even heavier. It drops a fraction and your shaking arms feel limp. Give in to fatigue? The question lurks for a long second. . . .

As concentration returns, so does determination. It *will* be two more reps. You summon the needed force by huffing and puffing out air and spittle. Your grip tightens on the knurled chrome. You lower the bar. The kiss becomes a solid thump and your glutes tighten and rise slightly. Halfway up, the bar falters and the center of your chest explodes into spasms of searing hot needles. Your eyes zero in on the bar as your hearing deserts you and the weight inches up to arm's length. You've crashed through the pain barrier with *one* more rep to go.

With legs twitching, kicking out to alleviate the pent-up electricity, you take three quick gasps for oxygen to see you through the last five seconds of agony. A whispered word from your training partner, "One more!", spirits through your mind to give you extra courage. Ominously the bar comes down for the final exertion, almost out of control. As it rams into your chest and bounces into orbit, a fleeting thought of failure strikes again, but is instantly killed in a burst of iron determination to finish the job . . . and the bar continues to climb. Your face catches fire, veins swell, temples pound, and with teeth-clenched courage, amid hellish pain shooting through your pectorals, you "growl" the weight skyward. As the elbows lock, the weight falls away into the welcome hands of a training partner; you stomp your feet rapidly on the floor to chase the pain from your body. It slides away and you curl up from the bench—the beastly "burn" has turned to wondrous warmth. The "pump" has arrived!

The beauty of bodybuilding is that you can change your appearance. By your own efforts you can add or subtract pounds of body weight. You can build your arms, shoulders, legs, chest, back, and in so doing, you can get a pleasure from training you might never have dreamed possible. Even the pain has its reward: It is invariably followed by the most desirable effect of all—the pump.

This book accompanies you through the motions you know so well already. In text and photographs, the world's most advanced hardcore bodybuilding techniques are discussed and dissected. I hope it will inspire you to go the extra distance to greatness.

Use this book to break out with new enthusiasm for your bodybuilding workouts and take yourself to higher plateaus of physical perfection. Greater success *can* be yours. Here are all the advanced techniques and principles to "force-feed" your muscles to titanic new dimensions.

You will always hear differing views on bodybuilding: Do's and don'ts that seem to contradict each other, eating suggestions that appear to conflict and exercise techniques that seem at odds. Don't worry about it.

Your body's growth depends on change. You have to surprise your muscles now and again, confuse them, pound them out. Progression is the whole point. Vary the intensity, the angle of approach, the workout length, the sets and reps—but always go for more, more, more. Don't, however, suddenly shift exercises, i.e., jump from, say, performing heavy squats right into vigorous thigh extensions without first warming up each area with light weights gradually. That can only lead to muscle tear.

This book contains the collective wisdom of the pros: sound advice, tumultuous techniques, flamboyant ideas, all designed to help you crash through your present sticking point. But nothing will happen unless you make it. Your development will reflect your total effort. Bring intensity, enthusiasm, regularity and courage to your training and you can't fail.

Accept the challenge to go all the way to bodybuilding stardom. Why not? You're young now. Life is fleetingly short. Make tonight's workout different from all previous ones. Make it your first step to real physical greatness. Is it trite to remind you that we live but once? This minute I want you to decide that you will push your limits, surpass your present point of development, venture on, on to that privileged spot at the top of the ladder—reserved one future day exclusively for you!

APPRECIATION

A book is not just the brainchild of one author. I owe a vote of thanks to many people:

First, to the bodybuilders themselves who appear within these pages. They are a great lot: Egos rise and fall, differences come and go, but it takes guts and determination to keep pumping iron, and that is the bond that unites us all. I respect each champion for bringing something unique to the sport.

To Pete Grymkowski and Tim Kimber of Gold's Gym and Joe Gold of World Gym, who run the two greatest hardcore bodybuilding establishments on earth, I extend heartfelt gratitude for your kindnesses.

Also, to International Federation of Bodybuilders (IFBB) head Ben Weider, whose openhouse policy keeps American bodybuilding healthy and vibrant, my respect and thanks, and to Joe Weider whose gift for publishing keeps our sport in front of the public. My appreciation to photographers Ralph DeHaan, Steve Douglas and Garry Bartlett, three talented photographers whose fresh approach to muscle camera art makes this book exciting. Special thanks to Al Antuck, Doris Barrilleaux, Chris Lund, Paula Crane, Denie Walters, Art Zeller, B&K Sports, John Balik, and Norberto Corriente for their contributions.

Eddie Robinson, just named Mr. USA.

CHAPTER 1

GENETICS

If you're in normal robust health, you'll find that regular weight training will bring pretty fast results. Even in the first weeks you will notice a difference in your muscle tone, strength and muscular development. As the weeks turn into months there tends to be a slowing down in your progress. This progress is dictated to a large extent by genetics. In other words, our natural ability to respond to progressive resistance exercise.

No one has an ideal genetic heritage, but obviously some people have a more natural reaction to progressive weight training than others. In the "old" days people would claim to be able to project potential at gaining muscle, simply by measuring bone size. For example, a six-inch wrist was considered *very* small, a six-and-a-half-inch wrist was small, a seven-inch wrist was normal, a seven-and-a-quarter would be slightly above normal, and a seven-and-a-half- or eight-inch wrist was considered to be superior. The thinking in those days was that the bigger the wrist the more able you were to gain muscular size. Although the size of our ankles, knees and wrists *are* an indication, in many cases, of our ability to gain muscular size, the skeletal structure is not the complete answer to being able to project one's potential for bodybuilding. For example, Serge Nubret has 21-inch arms, but he also has wrists under seven inches in thickness. This was considered unheard of in the past, because arms of such enormous size usually occurred on people who had wrists of more than eight inches in circumference.

Men like Arnold Schwarzenegger, Lou Ferrigno, Sergio Oliva, Mike Christian, Eddie Rob-

Multi-Olympic winner Frank Zane taught bodybuilders the meaning of the word "ripped."

inson, Bertil Fox, all have arms of over 20 inches and all have wrists of about seven and a half inches or thereabouts.

Today we try and judge the genetic values of a body by other means than looking at the relative thickness of the bones. To be a successful bodybuilder today you need at least some degree of body shape. That means that the shoulder clavicles should be quite wide, the hip and pelvic area should be relatively narrow, the bones of the legs should be straight. In addition to this, there should be relatively natural good peak to the biceps, a full-bodied look to the triceps. (The triceps shouldn't be really high up near the shoulder, they should have a lot of triceps cells lower down the arm, nearer the elbow.) The thighs shouldn't be excessively large up near the pelvis. There should be plenty of cells and aptitude for building muscle in the lower regions of the thigh, so that the vastus internus and vastus externus, (the lower quads) will be able to develop good sweep. The calves must have a low belly and a natural diamond shape so that when they're built they'll look impressive.

Things like the abdominals do not necessarily have to be straight, but if the lines and ridges of the abdominals form an even line it *does* improve the visual aspect to some extent. The back should have plenty of cells and the scapula, that is the shoulder blades, should be relatively mobile so that they can be pulled out to form that all-important "V" shape. Genetics are an important part of bodybuilding if you're aiming to become a Mr. Universe or even a national champion, because there are so many people with good genetics, that those with poor genetics don't really stand a chance even if their work ethic and determination are extremely high. In the old days people like Larry Scott and Frank Zane were considered to have had less than perfect genetics for bodybuilding but the word was out that they had "beaten" genetics, and still became champions by training intelligently. Today, I think it's fair to say, champions like Rich Gaspari do not have ideal genetics for winning a Mr. Olympia contest; yet in spite of having narrow shoulders and a relatively blocky physique Gaspari has thrilled the world with what he's done with his body, a result of course, of his enormous determination and willingness to give everything to his sport.

It is the muscle cells, the amount of them, that limits our ultimate development. If we have an abundance of cells in the various muscle areas, then our weight training will project faster results than if we had only small amounts of cells. Medical authorities tell us that the number of cells we have at birth do not change during our lifetime. This is now being debated heatedly by some people in the medical profession.

Who has the best genetics in bodybuilding? Well, of course we can't say for sure but I think it's safe to state that some of the most superb genetics were allocated to Sergio Oliva, Steve Reeves, Danny Padilla, Eddie Robinson, Cory Everson, Sandy Ridell, Lee Haney and the amazing Bob Paris.

While bones don't tell the whole story by any means, they are at least a pretty good indicator of our potential for bodybuilding. With regular hard workouts most men might be able to obtain a muscular upper arm measurement 10 inches above their wrist size. In the case of women, most might be able to build an arm seven inches above their wrist size.

One of the secrets of building muscle is the amount of circulating testosterone we have in our blood. Both men and women have levels of testosterone. Since it is the male hormone, it is only natural that men have more of this substance than women. This gives them an advantage when it comes to building muscle mass. It is also a known fact that those with high levels of testosterone tend to have lower levels of fat on the body.

We all know that athletes from all walks of life can improve their performance by taking additional dosages of testosterone. Fortunately today, most competitive sports have drug testing procedures which alert the athletes to the fact that they can't load up as they did in the pre-testing years. Today dope testing is very sophisticated and virtually all foreign substances can be detected. Accordingly, athletes

Bob Paris in the relaxed side pose.

Francis Benfatto—one of the world's most perfect bodies.

can be banned from the various sports that they are partaking in. Scientists are finding out that male hormone production can be stimulated naturally without the use of anabolic steroids by various processes. Regular sunshine can increase male hormone production. It is also a fact that regular vigorous exercise (squats) can induce higher levels of testosterone. There were some scientific experiments made during the last decade that indicated that testosterone levels could be increased when a so-called healthy diet was followed, as opposed to one that contained junk foods. In a nutshell, this would translate as those following a diet of natural fruits, fibres, vegetables, cereals and whole grains would benefit more than others who followed a diet of foods such as sugar-and-fat-loaded candies, cookies, doughnuts, and the like.

One interesting factor with regard to genetics is that one can be born with a potential for building an impressive physique in only one part of the body and not another. Many men and women find that they respond well to arm exercises or leg exercises yet fail to notice much difference in their backs and chests. Others may find that their shoulders grow very easily, while at the same time, their calves are almost impossible to improve. Tom Platz, a well known figure in bodybuilding, has enormous potential for building size in his legs, yet has difficulty building other areas such as his shoulders and arms. Bertil Fox has outrageously large arms yet his "V" taper of the back is less than ideal. Gary Strydom has amazing chest, shoulder, and leg muscles, while his back thickness fails to impress.

Underpar calf development has been the downfall of many male and female bodybuilders. It often seems that whatever they did, however hard they trained, they were unable to improve either the shape or the size of their lower legs. Many black men have found that while they have enormous aptitude for building an impressive back, large arms, or an imposing chest, building up their calves is extremely difficult. Many black men's and women's lower legs are typified by a high calf muscle which will not grow in size and this can hinder their overall placing in bodybuilding contests. One might be tempted to say that this should not interfere with their placings in the contest because there's nothing they can do to correct the disproportion. However, it is also true that other races have their problems with regard to bodybuilding genetics. For example, the East Indian tends to have very long, thin arms, and in the vast majority of cases the building of a 19-, 20- or 21-inch arm is totally unrealistic. Furthermore, Asians often have thick knees and ankles which take away from the accepted bodybuilding aesthetics that form an important part of our judging criteria.

Having mentioned these various trends of certain races, I hasten to say that my comments should not be taken as a putdown of any one race or nation. Certainly, examples of black men with superb calf development exist in the physiques of Chris Dickerson, Johnny Fuller, Bertil Fox, Sergio Oliva, and Lee Haney. In a similar vein, Prem Chand of India has enormously thick arms with good shape that can compete

Even when relaxed, the mighty muscles of Bertil Fox are awesome.

on equal terms with any other pair of arms on earth.

The ideal genetics for a bodybuilder hoping to go as far as he can on the competition stage would be to have a large amount of cells in all bodyparts, long insertions and origins of the muscle. That is to say, long muscles are preferred over short muscles. A "high" calf or a "high" triceps is less desirable than a "low" calf or a "low" triceps. A thigh that has most of its development near the upper part is not regarded as genetically advantaged. Those with wide shoulders and a narrow pelvis are at an advantage over those who have narrow shoulders and boxy hips.

The interesting thing about genetics, especially those who have genetic advantages, is that many of these people don't have the other ingredients for success, and therefore, in spite of having advanced or superior genetics they fail to achieve anything in the bodybuilding field, simply because they cannot dedicate themselves to training hard and eating correctly. On the other hand, as I mentioned earlier, there are those with certain body parts that don't respond well, those whose genetics are less than ideal, who with determined concentration on training and a dedication towards keeping good dietary habits have broken the barriers of development. However, it is generally understood that our limitations are determined by our forebears. One small comfort is that as yet no one has utilized his physical potential to the full limits of his capacity.

Laura Creavalle likes the 45° triceps stretch.

Most muscle strains or tears repair themselves within a week or two, but training has to be halted or reduced so that the injury doesn't worsen. Unfortunately, all athletes and bodybuilders injure themselves from time to time. These injuries vary from minor back tears, shoulder sprains and tendonitis to major injuries such as pectoral and biceps rips where the muscle actually tears away from the bone. All injuries are regrettable because they take away from your training time. Often one can "train around" a minor injury. This means that if you've injured your shoulder, for example, you could still probably be able to work the legs, chest, arms, and back by carefully selecting exercises that didn't work the injured area.

Major injuries are a different matter—they require immediate surgery. People like Berry DeMey, Johnny Fuller, Rich Gaspari, Chris Dickerson, John Brown, and Sly Stallone have ripped their pectoral muscles badly. Tom Platz, Al Beckles, Lou Ferrigno and Joe Bucci have incurred biceps injuries. In Platz's case he waited almost a year before having surgery. He had bad advice. Most surgeons today say that surgery should be immediate if full recovery is to be expected.

CHAPTER 2
WARMING UP

Warmups are important if we want to avoid injury. The most common single cause of injury is egotism. As Bob Paris says, "You should hang your ego on the gym door." Weight trainers, especially beginners, are often tempted to have a go at a weight that is just too heavy. You may well be able to perform lateral raises with 40-pound dumbbells, but never be tempted to go for the 60's just because your

David Baglivo gives some resistance to Joe Bucci (Mr. World) at Gold's Gym, Venice, California.

workout partner can handle them with ease. Move up to the 45's and then the 50's. In due course you will get to the 60's. It may take awhile but at least you'll get there injury-free. I have made many training mistakes that have caused injury. One was trying to deadlift a weight that was 200 pounds more than I had done before. It went up halfway, and that was the end of my lower back. Well, not quite, but I was out of circulation for the better part of a month! Another time I tried to jerk press a heavy dumbbell overhead. Leaning to one side I managed to get it to arm's length. After I had returned the weight to the floor I noticed a numbness in my neck, traps and deltoid. I had caused a pinched nerve condition which stayed with me for a year!

But my biggest training mistake ever was my 10-year devotion to improving my strength in two pursuits. As a youngster I had always been fascinated by wrist wrestling. I would take on anyone, anywhere, anytime. I wrist wrestled at shows and entered every tournament I could find. I rigged up a variety of pulley machines, some of which used free weight resistance while others utilized heavy rubber or steel strands—all to help me improve my wrist wrestling ability. What I *didn't* know was that this sport puts tremendous pressure on the elbow joint and the surrounding connective tissue. I should have known I was doing myself harm when the dull ache of elbow tendonitis stayed with me for days after each tournament.

The other strength pursuit that fascinated me was the single-arm chin. I would practice and practice to no avail. I once read that when you can perform 29 two-arm chins, you should have the strength to perform a one-arm chin. And although I got my two-arm chins up to 35, I still couldn't master the one-arm variation. But I didn't fail to try. I would hang on the horizontal bar with one hand and hold my wrist with my free hand. I would add weight to my body. And train for hours at a time. All to no avail. Then one day while training in Florida with John Mese I met a young bodybuilder. His name was Gino. Seeing me hanging by one arm on the chin bar, he asked me what I was trying to do. I told him that it was my ambition to perform a one-arm chin. He had never heard of the movement. After I explained he tried it out, and to my utter amazement performed *five* consecutive repetitions. And he performed them almost effortlessly. And here I was trying for ten years and never knowing success.

It wasn't until considerably later that I

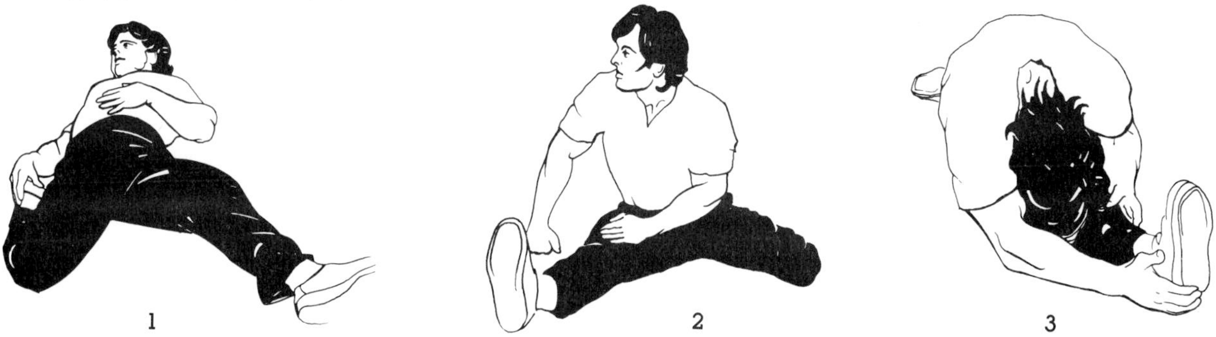

Stretch exercise.

found out that neither wrist wrestling nor one-arm chin attempts were healthy exercises for the elbows. Last year I had extensive elbow surgery to repair the damage done by the physical abuse I had inflicted on my right elbow during the years of my reckless disregard for sensible training.

There are three ways of warming up in bodybuilding. One is to warm up the overall physical motor—heart, lungs and general circulation. Ideally, before embarking on a vigorous workout you should start with a few minutes of stretching, rope jumping or running in place. This will get your heart pumping strongly and your blood coursing through your veins. After that kind of warming up, you really feel like working out.

Stretching is extremely important in preventing and treating some weight-training injuries. Bodybuilders are not always sure which specific stretching exercises are best, though.

It is a good idea to perform the following mini-routine of stretching before beginning any exercises. Do them with smooth, gliding motions—do not bounce or tug doing any of them. Only those stretches that you repeat regularly will prove beneficial. All stretches should be done ten times, always holding the position till the count of 10.

If you find it difficult to perform any of these stretching movements, simply try your best and go through the motions. Your mobility will gradually improve, as will the effectiveness of your regular workout training. In a roundabout way, stretching will help you get the most from your weights.

Stretch Exercise: Position #1

Adopt the lay-back position shown, gently stretching the frontal thigh muscles by bringing your ankle back to touch the back of your hips. Do not force the position or jerk the limbs. Follow the same procedure with the other leg.

Stretch Exercise: Position #2

Attempt to do a split, placing your legs as near as you can get to this position without straining. Place your hands on the floor to alleviate strain on the hamstrings.

Stretch Exercise: Position #3

Staying in the position adopted in the previous stretch, Position #2, attempt to slowly lower your head onto your knee, while also pulling your heel downwards away from you.

A third, and equally important, form of warming up is doing at least one light warmup set of each exercise before going on to attempt near-limit poundages for a certain number of repetitions. This not only safeguards the muscles but also the tendons and joints. The human body is capable of incredible power and athletic performance, but it is an extremely sensitive and delicate machine, *especially* in a highly trained athlete, or an individual dedicated to pushing to new physical plateaus.

The irony is that your untrained brother,

Ken "Flex" Wheeler.

father, or mother may run for a bus or otherwise exert themselves, and suffer *no* after-effects from the effort. You, on the other hand, try the same thing and get a charley horse. Have you ever noticed champion runners suddenly pulling up with injuries during a race? The average *untrained* man may not be as fast but he wouldn't have so many tears and sprains.

Why? Simply because a finely tuned engine such as your body in top training is more susceptible to the hazards of breakdown. If it is not pampered and carefully tuned, it will not perform efficiently, and if totally neglected can even stop functioning.

As a bodybuilder, especially nearing peak condition, if you do not always warm up each body part thoroughly, you will sooner or later suffer a training injury which can set back your program anywhere from a few days to many months or even years.

Warmups become increasingly important as you gain size and strength. Warming up is also absolutely necessary for those who are getting on in years.

A famous bodybuilder who trained at a gym I frequented was such an enthusiast that if he was anywhere in the neighborhood he would have to pop in to chat. More often than not on these occasions, he would "jump in" on someone bench pressing and pound out as many reps as he could, without taking his jacket off! Several times he did this, completely cold, fully dressed: He'd jump in on the bench and pound out some reps, often with over 300 pounds. I could never understand how he could do it without warming up. Then one day it happened. Rrr-ii-p! He tore his pectoral muscle from sternum to shoulder. After a lengthy recuperation period he was back in training, but with a difference. *Now* he warms up.

You should warm up with each exercise you do. If, for example, you normally barbell-curl 100 pounds for 10 reps, then perform a set of 10 to 15 reps with about half that weight. A warmup should not be so easy that the muscle is *not* stimulated to really work, nor should it be so demanding as to spoil your muscles for the "quality" sets to come.

There is particular danger in changing exercises around. If, for example, you are used to performing overhead presses and lateral raises *prior* to heavy bench work, it would *not* be a good idea to suddenly perform the chest exercises *before* the shoulder routine. It could result in a nasty deltoid tear which would affect just about all your upper body training.

There are several really tricky moves in bodybuilding you have to watch out for: *Never* lift a loaded bar from the squat racks unless you are completely beneath it, both feet flat on the ground and evenly spaced, back flat.

Another no-no: Do not make a habit of regularly performing really heavy sets of barbell bent-over rowing. It's better to use a T-bar unit, or even safer, a single dumbbell while propping up the body (and back) with your free hand on a bench. Seated single-arm curls can also cause a back problem. Beware of lifting too much weight.

Squats, especially if you lean too far forward, also can strain the lower back. Never bounce when in the full squat position. Merely lower slowly into the bent-knee position (thighs parallel to the floor) and rise quickly. Bouncing deeply could sooner or later wreck both your lower back *and* your knees.

Although relatively easy to avoid if good sense is used, training injuries are nevertheless very common. Eighty percent of all bodybuilders suffer a training injury within a twelve-month period. Fifteen percent are currently in the throes of an injury.

When you injure yourself the best thing to do is to apply ice to the immediate area as soon as possible. Cease all exercise and rest the area. The next day you may massage the area with your fingertips.

Be especially wary of returning to full-fledged exercise, and do not perform the movement which caused the injury in the first place. Never perform any exercise that causes even the slightest aggravation to your injury. This will worsen the strain. It is good to find an exercise that works the approximate area that *doesn't* cause pain.

As an example, assume you hurt your shoulder doing heavy bench presses (you didn't warm up sufficiently). You may find you cannot do flying exercises, bench presses or even incline bench work. But, glory be, there is no pain when you do decline bench presses. So, rather than avoid all the chest exercises, you should do decline bench presses. You will find that working *around* the injury in this way will actually help the recovery cycle and keep the muscle area toned up.

The question of rupture or herniation often occurs to beginning weight trainers. Could it happen? Yes, but it's unlikely. I can recall only one, of all the top bodybuilders, ever rupturing himself while training. It is far more likely that you will rupture yourself by a sudden sneeze or cough than by following a regular regimen of pumping iron. Keeping injury free is difficult. But you should follow my suggestions if you want to avoid the problems of injury to the best of your ability. One last time. Don't jump your poundage up dramatically. And never "try your strength" or show off in front of others. The result can be just too costly. I know.

Monumental Vince Taylor trains his triceps in the pressdown.

How often should I train? How many times a week should I work my muscles? These are questions that are regularly asked by beginners, intermediaries, and even advanced trainers who want to exercise in the most efficacious manner possible. The answer is that you should train as frequently as possible without throwing your body into a sticking point, because of overtraining or failure to repair broken-down muscle cells. It is true that the more frequently you train, the faster your progress in bodybuilding will be, but with the proviso that you fully recuperate between workouts.

CHAPTER 3 WORKOUT FREQUENCY

It is generally agreed that a muscle that has been progressively trained takes at least 48 hours to fully recover. In some cases, this time span extends to 56 hours. This means you should not specifically train a muscle in an isolated fashion for at least a 48-hour period. Recuperation with bodybuilding workouts takes longer than recuperation from other activities. For example, runners, or people who have developed endurance skills; or field athletes, golfers or football players may not need a 48 hour period to recover from their practices but it is generally known that bodybuilding activity does require plenty of rest time for the muscles to recuperate.

Weight training is the most arduous way to work the body's muscles known to man. For example, if you lift a 100-pound barbell 20 times, you have, in a period of 20 odd seconds, lifted some 2000 pounds! Few other sports put this massive type of stress on the muscular system.

Beginners, as I have suggested already, should train just 3 times per week, working the entire body at each training session, and resting at least one full day between workouts. The advanced or intermediate bodybuilders often feel that training the whole body in one workout isn't practical. The beginner can do it easily because he will only be performing one set of each exercise in the beginning and this may graduate to 2 or even 3 sets per exercise. This in itself does not constitute a long workout since only 8 to 10 exercises will be involved.

The more advanced trainer may want to perform more sets (3 to 5 is average for the seasoned bodybuilder) and in most cases he or she may opt to include 2 or 3 exercises for each bodypart. It's not difficult to see that this lengthens the workout considerably. Whereas the beginner will find that a workout will only take 30 to 40 minutes, the experienced bodybuilder with his added exercises and sets may well find that the workout can take up to three hours. What is the answer? Well it certainly isn't to stay in the gym for three or four hours at a time. That would constitute almost living in the gym, and having no time for your family or friends. You may find that workouts are not only taking up all spare time but that you are unable to maintain a good pace from beginning to end. It is easy to run out of gas when you are lifting weights continuously during an arduous training session.

What is the solution? You should *split* your exercises into two or three parts. The simplest way to divide your program is to save all the upper body exercises for one training session and then utilize all the lower body exercises (legs) in another session. Alternatively some bodybuilders like to do what is known as pulling movements on one day (rowing, curls, chins, etc.) and all pushing movements (presses, triceps extensions, and squats) on another. My own preference is to work chest, back, and arms on one day, and legs, shoulders, and abdominals on the other days.

When you split your routine you can work out two successive days or more in a row because you are not working the same muscle groups each day. One day you may be working chest and legs, and the next day the back and arms will come in for their share of the routine. Generally speaking, your recuperative system can cope with this type of training. What it finds difficult to withstand is the working of the *same* muscle group on two consecutive days. This, therefore, is something to avoid.

There is a degree of overlap in training because many exercises work several different muscle groups at one time; however, this doesn't seem to interfere with recuperation too much. It is the concentrated performance of isolating exercises that interferes with recuperation. For example, it's not a good idea to perform chins on one workout day followed by curls on the next workout day because both exercises vigorously work the biceps muscle and this would interfere with recuperation. On the other hand, you could work the back muscles with chins on one day, and include the biceps work in that same workout. The next day you might concentrate more on exercises such as press behind neck and bench presses.

As I suggested before, you can actually split the workout on three consecutive days. Normally, you would choose to rest on the fourth day. This system is known as the *three-day-on-one-day-off* frequency system. It is very popular with many bodybuilders, and is, in fact, the most used form of frequency among the champions of our sport.

It should be noted that in off-season training (when you train without a contest in mind) the body will grow very well from just two training sessions per muscle group, each week. For example, if you work the calves, chest, back, etc., twice per week, you will be doing the right thing to make substantial gains in mass building. On the other hand, if a contest is in sight or if you have a set date at which you want to reach a peak for a photo session or a guest posing spot, then it is a good idea to increase the number of workouts you give a bodypart from two times a week to three times a week.

Anja Shreiner gives a hand to multi-Olympia winner Cory Everson.

FREQUENCY VARIATIONS OF THE SPLIT ROUTINE

Monday	Tuesday	Wednesday	Thursday	Friday	Saturday	Sunday
Upper Body	Lower Body	Upper Body	Lower Body	Upper Body	Lower Body	Rest
Upper Body	Lower Body	Rest	Upper Body	Lower Body	Rest	Rest
Upper Body	Lower Body	Upper Body	Rest	Lower Body	Upper Body	Rest
Lower Body	Upper Body	Lower Body	Rest	Upper Body	Lower Body	Rest
Upper Body	Lower Body	Upper Body	Lower Body	Rest	Rest	Rest
Lower Body	Upper Body	Lower Body	Upper Body	Rest	Lower Body	Upper Body
Lower Body	Upper Body	Rest	Lower Body	Upper Body	Lower Body	Upper Body
Upper Body	Rest	Lower Body	Rest	Upper Body	Rest	Lower Body
Chest, Delts, Upper Back, Triceps, Abs, Forearms	Thighs, Calves, Lower Back, Biceps	Same as Monday	Same as Tuesday	Same as Monday & Wednesday	Same as Tuesday & Thursday	Rest
Chest, Back, Delts, Calves, Abs, Forearms	Abs, Thighs, Arms	Same as Monday	Same as Tuesday	Same as Monday & Wednesday	Same as Tuesday & Thursday	Rest
Thighs, Back, Abs, Forearms, Biceps	Chest, Delts, Triceps, Abs, Calves	Same as Monday	Same as Tuesday	Same as Monday & Wednesday	Same as Tuesday & Thursday	Rest
Delts, Biceps, Forearms, Calves	Chest, Back, Legs, Abs	Same as Monday	Same as Tuesday	Same as Monday & Wednesday	Same as Tuesday & Thursday	Rest
Chest, Back, Delts	Biceps, Triceps, Forearms	Thighs, Calves	Same as Monday	Same as Tuesday	Same as Wednesday	Rest
Chest, Back, Calves, Abs	Delts, Biceps, Triceps, Abs	Thighs, Calves, Forearms	Same as Monday	Same as Tuesday	Same as Wednesday	Rest
Chest, Back, Arms	Legs, Waist	Delts	Same as Monday	Same as Tuesday	Same as Wednesday	Rest
Delts, Arms	Legs, Waist	Chest, Back	Same as Monday	Same as Tuesday	Same as Wednesday	Rest
Chest, Arms	Back, Delts	Legs, Waist	Same as Monday	Same as Tuesday	Same as Wednesday	Rest
Chest, Delts, Triceps, Abs	Rest	Thighs, Calves, Back, Biceps	Rest	Chest, Delts, Triceps, Abs	Rest	Rest
Thighs, Calves, Back, Biceps	Rest	Chest, Delts, Triceps, Abs	Rest	Thighs, Calves, Back, Biceps	Rest	Rest

Monday	Tuesday	Wednesday	Thursday	Friday	Saturday	Sunday
Chest, Abs, Calves	Delts, Arms	Rest	Thighs, Back, Abs	Chest, Calves, Abs	Rest	Delts, Arms, Abs
Thighs, Back, Abs	Rest	Chest, Calves, Abs	Delts, Arms, Abs	Rest	Thighs, Back, Abs	Chest, Calves, Abs
Legs, Triceps, Glutes	Chest, Biceps, Forearms	Shoulders, Back, Traps, Abs	Rest	Same as Monday	Same as Tuesday	Same as Wednesday

However, this can easily put your body into a non-gaining mode simply because you can easily fall into the trap of overtraining each muscle. When a muscle is overtrained, it becomes flat-looking, often stringy, weak, and certainly it will not grow in size. An overtrained muscle falls into a "sticking point" in which no progress is made. When we overtrain we actually invite further problems because there is a tendency to lose interest in training itself or to injure the muscles; consequently, we border on giving up training altogether.

A very workable routine which has increased in popularity during the 90's is the *every-other-day-split method*. In this system of frequency you perform one half of your workout one day, followed by a complete rest day. Then the second half of the workouts is performed on the next day, followed again by another rest day. This system is then repeated. At no time do you train two days in a row. Each half of the routine is followed by a complete day's rest. It is not difficult to see that following this system you train each bodypart one and a half to two times per week. Obviously, this system does not fit neatly into a seven-day cycle. It is strictly for home trainers or those who have access to gyms which are open seven days a week. The *every-other-day-split* is probably the most ideal training format for those whose recuperation is less than perfect. It is also a system which lends itself well to high-intensity workouts or workouts that are built up of lots of heavy exercises and quality sets.

Arnold Schwarzenegger has seemingly proved that one can train twice a day for six days a week and make progress in size and shape, but even "The Oak" himself could only do this for a limited period of time. His usual practice was to train just once a day, but he did train for two months prior to his contest—twice a day, six days a week.

Tonya Knight begins the triceps pressdown.

It is generally believed that recuperation is helped by good nutrition and adequate rest and general leisure in the fresh air and sunshine. This may be one reason why Californian bodybuilders seem to make better progress than others. They have fresh air and sunshine 350 days a year.

Training frequency is a vital factor in your bodybuilding success, but needs a little thought. Obviously, the amount of training you do has to fit in with your social life, your family commitments, your individual capacity for strenuous exercise, and your recuperative ability. Shown here are some frequency patterns that have proved successful for bodybuilders around the world.

François Muse shows the dumbbell variation of the rowing exercise.

One of the most fascinating things to me is trying to answer the question of how many sets and reps you should perform. This question is asked all the time by aspiring bodybuilders. They want to know exactly how many sets, how many repetitions they should perform, and in addition they want to be told what exercise style to use. I have made a long study of this particular situation and after many years I have concluded that there is no single ideal number of sets or reps that one should use to maximize progress. I am, however, certain that those who believe in performing very low sets, even though the intensity may be amazingly high, are making a mistake if they think they can build a championship calibre physique by following this method.

CHAPTER 4
SETS, REPS, AND CORRECT FORM

In a similar vein, I am convinced that there is no ideal number of repetitions that one should perform to maximize potential, nor do I believe that you should follow a single specific style of training. There are those in the sport that feel that every rep of every set should be *felt*, that the contraction should be found in the muscle prior to starting the repetition and should again be held and felt and identified at the conclusion of each repetition. Still others believe in cheating with all repetitions on every exercise. They believe implicitly that the more weight they use the faster the progress will be as a result of using that weight, even though it translates to having to use a loose exercise style. Often these people bounce the weight on their chests while doing bench presses, or lean back excessively while trying to push a weight overhead. Others will bounce while coming out of a deep squat or lean back excessively while performing the barbell curl. And then there are those who believe in high repetition pumping action. They neither use heavy weights nor concentrate on feeling the contraction. These people merely move the weight up and down in a fast pumping action so that blood is forced into the muscle being worked.

Which of these three methods is the best? My answer is all of them. I genuinely believe that the ultimate physical development will come about from the practice of using heavy weights, from using light pumping action methods, and from trying to utilize perfect style and feeling the contraction in every single repetition. Each method will bring about its own type of muscular development. For example, the muscle cell itself is built while performing progressively heavier and heavier sets using either more repetitions and heavier weight, or by taking less rest time between the sets.

A distinct advantage is also gained from those who endeavor to feel the contraction at the beginning and end of a movement. These people consciously squeeze the muscle while they are exercising. Each repetition is not an effort to raise the weight up, but is an attempt to make the muscle *feel* the resistance, so that it is maximally exhausted. The third procedure is to utilize a fast pumping action. This will tend to build the mitochondria which form 10 to 15 percent of the muscle mass that we build. It is easy to see, therefore, that those who concentrate on heavy weights only will miss out on the added muscle tissue that comes about from utilizing the pumping action that builds the mitochondria or the added refinement and shape that comes from *feeling* the muscular contraction during each repetition.

Bob Paris who is known for his perfect exercise style feels that every repetition of every set should be performed with a "feel" for the contraction. He has a saying: "Hang your ego on the gym door," which puts his philosophy in a nutshell. On the other hand, Mike Mentzer was noted for his single-minded dedication to the principle of adding weight to the bar in order to increase muscle size. Mike often quoted medical sources showing that increase of workload leads to increase of muscle mass. True enough, but scientific studies don't always include the knowledge acquired by modern bodybuilding exponents. If you watch most champions train, you will see that they vary greatly in the way in which they attack their workouts. Some workouts will be heavy because the champs have a gut feeling they should be performing a heavy workout. On these days you will notice them doing heavy squats or heavy bench press or heavy rows, etc. On other days, they will not feel the need to use mammoth poundages, so, instinctively, these champions will use lighter weights and become "feelers." At other times these same champions will employ the pumping method to put blood into the muscle so that it is fed with the essential nutrients. This method had recently been identified and named "pumping blood." Greg Zulak wrote a very interesting article in *MuscleMag International* which was received very well by the bodybuilding community and many champions acknowledged that Greg's writings were right-on, saying that they themselves had been following similar systems on a regular basis.

The body thrives on variety, and this is why I think a bodybuilder who is trying to make the most of his or her physique should try and develop an instinctive *feel* for training. You should become an expert on your own body, and learn how to read and understand what your body is telling you. Obviously you need constant stimulation to keep your muscles growing, but this stimulation comes about from the variety of training methods, rather than any one particular principle. For one thing, if you train heavy all the time, merely trying to get a weight from A to B, going to failure in each set, you will soon burn out and put the body into shock. This will result in zero growth. On the other hand, those who perform only muscle pumping exercises will find that the body soon yearns for more substantial weights. Likewise, those who utilize a perfect exercise form finding the contraction in every repetition, also come to realize that something is missing from their workouts.

Look back into the past. Arnold Schwarzenegger, Franco Columbu, Reg Park, Dave Draper, and even some of our more recent champions, devoted considerable time to power training. That is to say, they trained with 6 to 8 sets of basic exercises such as bent-over rows, presses, squats, using low repetitions on the 5 to 6 scale and hoisting as heavy a weight as they possibly could. This had the effect of building a foundation to their physiques. Today, these same men seldom use extremely heavy weights, but there is little doubt in their minds that the heavy training they did in their formative bodybuilding years helped them build a base for future bodybuilding success.

I strongly believe in performing repetitions over a very wide range from 5 to 50. Certain muscle groups such as the abdominals, forearms, calves, and even the thighs respond extremely well to high-repetition training. As Vince Gironda, the "Iron Guru," would say, they are "high-rep" muscles. There is no reason at all why you shouldn't take your squats into the 30 to 50 rep range. This holds for any muscle group. Do not limit yourself to only performing 8 to 12 repetitions which is so commonly advocated, in the various bodybuilding journals of today. My only proviso with regard to cheating is that you do not injure yourself by trying to hoist up weights beyond your natural ability. I feel that it is wrong to bounce a heavy weight on the sternum, for example. You could easily crack the bony area of the chest and damage yourself severely. Likewise, if you bounce continuously while performing heavy squats, you can injure the knees and the lower back to an extent that complete repair is impossible. Cheating should take the form of *creative* cheating. In other words, utilize loose form at a time when it can increase the breakdown of muscle cells. It is a good idea to cheat with an exercise at the stage when you can no longer perform a strict repetition. This will serve to break down more muscle cells than if you had stopped when you reached the positive failure mode.

Aaron Baker has his own version of the lat machine pressdown. He works one arm at a time.

The mighty Nimrod King.

When I was a kid in the 1960's and very keen on bodybuilding, I read up on everything I possibly could on the sport. I would be in awe of the massive poundages reported to be used by the various champions of the day. However, my eyes were really opened when I saw how most champions really trained. It seemed that the biggest and most successful bodybuilders did not train with super heavy weights. Neither did they use excessively light weights, but over the years it was obvious to me that the success of most bodybuilders was due to their performing of *lots of sets and reps using moderate weights*. Typically, I would see a bodybuilder using 10 to 15 sets per bodypart, utilizing somewhere between 10 to 15 repetitions, but always using moderate weights. Very seldom did I see a successful bodybuilder using excessively heavy weights in his or her exercises. Occasionally, on the basic movements I would see bodybuilders performing a few heavy sets to keep their muscles and tendons strong, but it was clear to me that most of the muscle size resulted from a system of high sets and medium to high repetitions utilizing moderate poundages. Typically, bodybuilders would use 35-pound dumbbells in their curls. Bench presses would be done utilizing 200 to 250 pounds only; press-behind necks, upright rows, were performed seldom using more than 120 pounds.

All this quite shocked me because my work ethic being very high at the time, I had striven to use as heavy a weight as I possibly could, and at 6′ in height, weighing around 200 pounds, I was able to press-behind neck 180 to 200 pounds for 10 repetitions. I could upright row with 160 pounds for 10 repetitions and squat with 350 pounds for 10 to 12 repetitions. I could chin myself a dozen times with a 50-pound dumbbell around my waist, and was able to curl 160 pounds for 12 reps. But, here I was observing other bodybuilders with 19- and 20-inch arms who were using far less poundage than myself, but with vastly superior development. It was then that I realized that the size of the weights used was relatively unimportant; in fact, heavy training with large weights can put an end to natural muscle growth. It is far better to coax the muscles into increased size by adding sets, and changing repetition patterns, than to stick to a system of trying to utilize heavier and heavier weights in each workout.

We live in an era of no pain, no gain. Does this saying apply to bodybuilding? My answer is yes and no. I believe that blasting through the pain barrier occasionally is important if ultimate muscle size is required. On the other hand, as I stated earlier, I believe that lower repetitions using heavy weights and *feeling* the contraction are also important. Larry Scott used to believe in a system of "burns." This method involves performing 3 to 5½ reps at the end of a set, to blast blood into the area that otherwise wouldn't be stimulated if the set was concluded at the time of normal fatigue. Typically, Scott would perform preacher bench curls for 8 or 9 repetitions, and then, at the top of the movement, when he couldn't do any more curls, he would do 5 or 6 quarter reps, which became known in bodybuilding terminology as "burns." Again, I believe there is some use for this type of training.

Gary Strydom doing side laterals.

Should you train slow or fast? My answer is both. Should you train using high reps or low reps? My answer is both. And again let me reiterate that I see no reason whatsoever why high and low reps, fast and slow reps, cheat or strict reps, or whatever, should not be incorporated into the same workout. In other words, you don't have to train for three or four months using heavy weights in a powerlifting mode. I see no reason why we shouldn't mix up our training styles in a single workout. In fact, there may be a definite benefit in keeping variety, because to utilize just one system might drive us into a state of boredom and increase the likelihood of bringing about a sticking point. Variety is the spice of life! Variety is the spice of bodybuilding!

As I write this in the 1990's, there is still a movement which propounds that the heavy-duty system of training is the only way to increase muscle mass. For example, the philosophy dictates that we can only gain and succeed in bodybuilding if we use extremely intense training, low sets, and excessive strain to achieve the rep goal. I categorically refuse to believe that this method is the way to championship muscles.

Glancing through a book on high-intensity training not long ago I was amazed at the pictures of the athletes illustrating the pages. Having seen 95 percent of these same athletes training, I knew that the muscles being displayed in this book were not built as a result of the recommended training procedures. Lots of reps, lots of sets, that is the answer.

I have never in my life seen a physique star who built his or her body utilizing one or two sets with all-out intensity. I believe that to promote this system as workable for the aspiring bodybuilding champion is a disservice to those who spend their hard-earned cash to learn the secrets of the champions. To merely increase the weight on an exercise you will accomplish one thing—you will get stronger; however, it will not take the muscles to the massiveness required for bodybuilding competition. If you doubt my words, check out the physiques of the strongest men and women in the world. Their muscles are rotund, but not by any stretch of the imagination, as shapely, or peaked, or as bulbous as those of the competitive bodybuilder. No lifter has the appearance of an Olympia winner. In an excellent article in *Muscle and Fitness* magazine entitled, "How to Build Muscle," Dr. Gold has pointed out that if you train with single reps or low repetitions for power the way many powerlifters do, you will get stronger than the average bodybuilder, who is performing 8 to 12 repetitions, but that this strength only applies to the performance of low repetitions. Dr. Gold states that you will probably gain less muscle mass than if you trained with additional repetitions and more feel for each count. He points out that runners or swimmers whose activities involve high repetitions do not build massive muscles because they do not overload their muscles in their workouts. "It takes a combination of muscular overload, plus additional blood flow to the muscles, to create the kind of hypertrophy that bodybuilders want," Dr. Gold advises. He's right. Variety is your key.

Darren James.

Every day thousands of newcomers enter the sport of bodybuilding. Many keep with their workouts no longer than three or four months. Others stay with it for a period of years. Only a few stay with it for life. But bodybuilding is a lifestyle that can, and in my opinion should be, practiced as long as one lives. Of course, we have to tailor our exercises to our age, our state of fitness and our natural tolerance level for strenuous physical exercise, but I have no doubt that sensible bodybuilding can be continued well into the later years.

CHAPTER 5
BEGINNER'S GAME PLAN

Beginners to bodybuilding are often impatient. They want fast, sure, safe gains in muscle size, strength, health and well-being. Quite frequently they don't get proper instruction at a gym, or they buy a set of weights without having any information on how to go about getting started. This is a mistake. One should always try to follow some sort of advice when getting into this sport. There are ground rules with regard to bodybuilding as there are with any sport. Starting out is a time when you should adhere to the specific advice of an expert. Accordingly, in this chapter I am going to give you some advice on how to get started in bodybuilding, and much of what I say will be specific in that I will dictate the exact amount of sets and reps you are to perform. The exercises I recommend are not to be interchanged with others.

At the beginning stage you must follow the rules of the game. It is not a time for you to experiment or try out different systems. After you have finished your initiation, then periods of experimentation can be utilized, but for now you as a beginner must follow the exact advice offered.

You may well find that other so-called experts in the field will offer you different combinations of exercises, sets, and repetitions. Remember, the shortest route is the correct route. If you choose the wrong path at the beginning of your journey, you may never reach your destination. It is my opinion that bodybuilding for the beginner must be simple. It must be basic. It must be short. Your job at this stage is to build a basis or a foundation for the ultimate physique that you eventually hope to create.

Successful bodybuilding depends on three aspects:

1. Vigorous progressive resistance exercise using free weights and free-weight machines.

2. Proper nutrition which serves the purpose of feeding the muscles and keeping the body and the various body processes in top working order.

3. Rest and sleep, to afford complete recuperation from workouts.

Keep these three aspects in mind at all times; each must be given your fullest attention. If you ignore any one, you will be hurting your chances for success.

Although there is always room for ideas and differing opinions in this sport, as there is in all sports, I am going to take the bull by the horns and insist that you stick to my advice here, at least in the beginning stages, and that you don't allow yourself to be influenced by what others say or by whatever else you may read. It will only serve to confuse you. Your apprenticeship is the time to follow *my* rules. Later, as you pass from the beginner's stage to the intermediate and then on to the advanced stage you will find that your experience and acquired knowledge will give you the right to experiment and use various forms of trial and error in your bodybuilding. For now, however, trust my knowledge, and I will get you through this important initial stage.

First off, before even starting bodybuilding, get a check-up from your doctor. Ask for a stress test, and a complete physical examination. Tell your doctor that you're taking up a program of vigorous bodybuilding. By all means show him this book. There is nothing to fear from a stress test. Your doctor will simply put you through some standard exercises to see how your heart and other organs function under physical exertion. The reason I'm asking you to go for a complete check-up is to make sure that if by chance you have a heart or other organic disorder your doctor may or may not give you the "all clear" for regular bodybuilding exercises. Chances are, your doctor will be delighted that you're undertaking a program of vigorous, healthy exercise. On the other hand, if some abnormality does show up you will be spared the aggravation of worsening the condition with strenuous exercise.

Bodybuilding is an athletic pastime, and you do have to be in robust health to benefit from the training. If you are over 35 years of age, or if you are a heavy drinker or smoker, or if you have not exercised formally since your school years, then I suggest you clean up your act now, before going for that stress test. You must follow basic, healthy rules of living if you hope to build an impressive, healthy physique.

Your exercise program consists of just eight movements. These are all you perform. Do not make the mistake of thinking that more exercises are necessarily better; do not change the order of the exercises listed; do not leave out movements; and do not increase training days. If you feel that your arms or legs or chest, etc., are extra skinny and need more work, do not add additional movements to these areas. Keep to my advice.

At the conclusion of this chapter I describe the eight exercises that make up the beginner's routine. Each exercise is to be performed for *one set*. That is to say you perform 8 to 10 repetitions one time only and then you stop that exercise. Pushing a barbell up and then lowering it is known as one repetition. Doing it again is known as 2 repetitions, 3 times is 3 repetitions . . . If you do, say, one series of 8 repetitions, this is known as 1 set of 8 reps (1×8).

Should you put the weight down after resting for a minute or two, and then do another set of 8 repetitions, this is known in the sport as 2 sets of 8 reps (2×8). In some cases, advance bodybuilders perform up to 10 or 12 sets of just one exercise, but the usual figure is between 3 and 5. You, as a beginner, are hereby instructed to perform just one set for the time being.

You will notice that the repetitions vary somewhat in the beginner's routine. This is because certain muscle groups are known as "high-rep" muscles. That is to say that they tend to respond better to higher repetition counts, than they do to the performance of lower repetitions.

The catalyst that makes bodybuilding exercises work is food. It's really quite simple. If you want to gain muscular body weight then you should increase the amount of food you eat. This translates as additional calories which serve to increase body weight. Should you want to reduce overall body weight, then limit your calorie intake (food) gradually to the extent that you are losing weight at about 1 or 2 pounds per week. Simple? Yes. I have devoted a chapter to nutrition in this book, and the advice therein applies to beginners as well as advanced bodybuilders.

As for the exercises themselves, they need to be performed exactly as I have indicated in the explanatory text. Additionally you should follow the form shown in the illustrations in each exercises.

Some important points to follow are:

- Do not fall into the trap of using sloppy or loose form.

- Do not lean back excessively, when pressing a weight overhead.

- Do not swing the bar up during a curling motion.

- Do not bounce down low in a squatting motion.

- Do not raise the hips and bounce the bar during the bench pressing movement.

Generally speaking, the beginner should avoid all forms of ballistic movements in training. Keep the exercise motion smooth and relatively slow. It is suggested that a weight be raised at the rate of 1½ to 2 seconds and lowered at a time span of about 3 to 4 seconds. This advice is for beginners only. There is some variation for more advanced trainers.

Rest and recuperation are important if you are going to make good progress in bodybuilding. Make sure that you get adequate sleep . . . 7, 8, or even 9 hours, depending on your individual needs. It is far better to get a regular 8 hours sleep each night, than go with only a few hours for several nights and then to try and make up the sleep by staying in bed most of the weekend. Excessive partying, together with smoking and drinking that often go with it, is most definitely not conducive to making steady bodybuilding progress.

Normally muscular gains in size and strength come at a fast rate for the beginner. Of course they may never come fast enough to completely satisfy you, but you will be pleasantly surprised if you keep up with your training. Do not expect overnight results. However, you could be very surprised when you look in the mirror after a few months to see that you have gained a significant amount of muscle mass and improved body shape and definition.

The following is a beginner's routine that you should perform three times a week with at least a day's rest between each workout. Perform this routine Monday, Wednesday and Friday, or Tuesday, Thursday, and Saturday, etc. Always make sure that your workout is followed by a day in which no weight training exercises are performed. Your muscles need a full day to "mend" themselves after heavy exercise.

Press-Behind-Neck
Squat
Bench Press
Wide-Grip Chins
Barbell Curl
Lying Triceps Extension
Standing Calf Raise
Crunches

Press-behind-neck (start).

Press-behind-neck (finish).

Wide-grip chin (start).

Wide-grip chin (finish).

Press-Behind-Neck

This is probably the all-time most popular movement for size building in the shoulder area. The lateral (side) head of the deltoid is worked most, although all three areas are exercised. Perform 8 to 10 repetition with a barbell weighing 40 to 50 pounds. Inhale before pushing up and exhale as the arms lock out.

When you get to the stage of being able to handle fairly hefty weights (about 130 pounds) you may take the weight from squat racks to make it easier to get to the initial behind-the-neck position. Some bodybuilders prefer to perform this exercise in the seated position. This eliminates any help that you might sometimes unconsciously use in the lift. Grip the bar so that your forearms can be vertical when the weight is resting on your shoulders. Perform your reps without pausing, and keep your back straight during the exercise. Although primarily a shoulder exercise, this movement also works the upper back, the trapezius and the triceps of the upper arm.

Wide-Grip Chins

A very important bodybuilding exercise, wide-grip chins are performed by just about every bodybuilding champion. Start by hanging from a high horizontal chin bar. Make sure that the lats are fully stretched and the arms are straight. Pull up strongly (keeping the elbows back) until the bar is behind your head. Lower and repeat. If you try to "concentrate" the effort into your lats, they will benefit. At first, you may find this exercise difficult to perform. Keep persevering. Aim ultimately for 12 to 15 reps even though at first you may only be able to perform 1 or 2 reps. Inhale before raising up, and exhale as the bar arrives behind your head.

The great benefit offered by this exercise is a wider back. There is a tendency for the scapula (shoulder blades) to be pulled outwards. There is also a long-term benefit to your shoulder width. In fact, the wide-grip chin helps lift the entire upper body.

Barbell curl (start).

Barbell curl (finish).

Barbell Curl

Stand with the legs comfortably apart, holding a barbell loaded to about 40 pounds. Your grip should be about shoulder width, or perhaps slightly wider. Without leaning back, take a deep breath and "curl" the barbell to the shoulders. Do not bend the knees. Try to raise the weight while keeping your elbows fairly close to your body. Exhale as the bar arrives at your shoulder level; lower and repeat. Try for 10 repetitions. This is the most basic of all biceps exercises and is the best one for building up that muscle.

Lying Triceps Extension

This exercise builds more size into the triceps than any other single movement. Lie on a flat bench, holding a moderately weighted barbell, with your hands from 2 to 10 inches apart. Keeping the upper arms vertical, raise the barbell up and down behind the head. Inhale before the lift. Exhale as the arms straighten. Try 8 to 10 reps.

Squat

The regular barbell squat is like the free-standing squat, with the addition of a loaded barbell across the back of your shoulders. It is great for the quadriceps. If you are very underweight, you may want to wrap a towel around the bar where it rests on the upper back to help prevent the bar from chafing your skin. It is important to keep your head up and your back flat during the entire movement. Starting poundages vary from 50 to 100 pounds depending on your present strength and condition. Many bodybuilders are able to squat with double their body weight. The best squatter of all time was Paul Anderson who, at 400 pounds, squatted once with 1,230 pounds!

One interesting aspect of squatting is that regular heavy squatting (say five sets of ten to fifteen reps) puts such demands on the system that invariably the metabolism reacts and growth of the entire body is stimulated. Some authorities actually claim that squatting causes the body to manufacture far more of its own natural steroids.

Crunches

Lie on the floor with your legs resting on top of an exercise bench, so that your thighs are in the vertical position. With your hands behind your head attempt to sit up. Lower and repeat. Breathe in before raising your upper body and exhale as you lower it. Crunches are good for the entire abdominal area.

Standing Calf Raise

This exercise gives the calves a good workout. It involves the simple process of rising up on your toes (lifting the heels). The resistance can be supplied by a special apparatus (a standing calf machine) or a heavy barbell across the shoulders. Use a block under the toes and rise up as high as possible. S-T-R-E-T-C-H. Go for 20 to 30 reps.

Bench Press

It doesn't take a genius to see that the bench-press movement is in fact an upside-down floor dip. But it is superior as a chest-building exercise because you do not have to hold your body straight, nor do you have to balance to the same extent. The most important factor is that you can add amounts of weight to the bar on a regular basis. In this way, the movement uses progressive resistance to build muscle steadily. Before you know it, you'll be handling respectable poundage in this exercise. Start with 40 to 60 pounds, and be prepared to handle 200 pounds or more within your first year of training. Inhale as you lower the weight; exhale as it goes up. (Imagine you are blowing it up.) Most people lower the weight to the nipple area, but those who wish to build "higher" pectorals may lower the bar to the upper chest. Do not under any circumstance allow the weight to bounce from the sternum (chest bone) as this could damage the delicate nerve center located beneath it.

When bench-pressing, grip so that the forearms are vertical when the bar is resting on the chest. Push the weight up to arm's length. Do not allow the weight to drop, but rather lower it with control to the original position. Perform between 4 to 15 reps (strength comes from 4 to 5 reps; muscle size comes from 6 to 15). The bench press has been nicknamed the king of the torso builders because of the growth-producing effect it has on the entire upper body.

Lying triceps extension (start).

Lying triceps extension (finish).

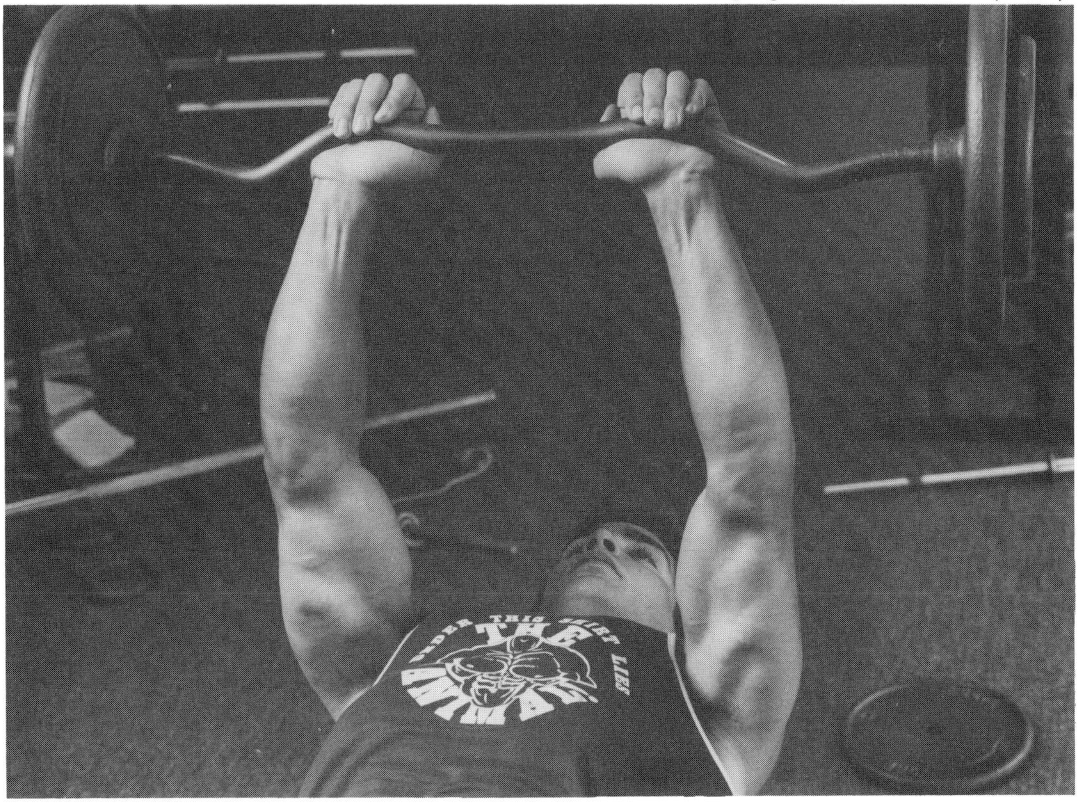

Squat (start).

Squat (finish).

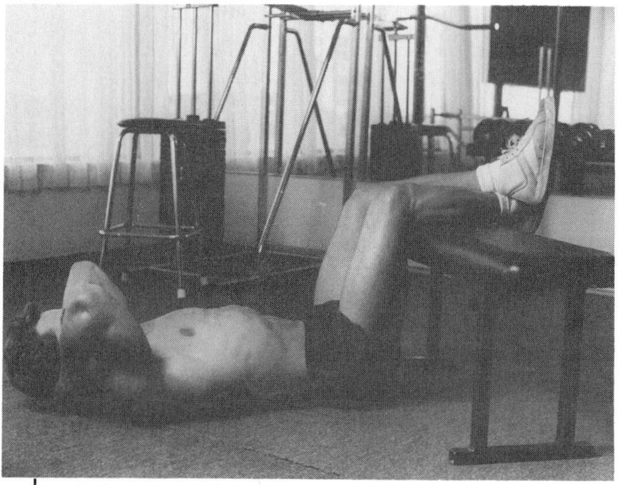

Crunches (start).

Crunches (finish).

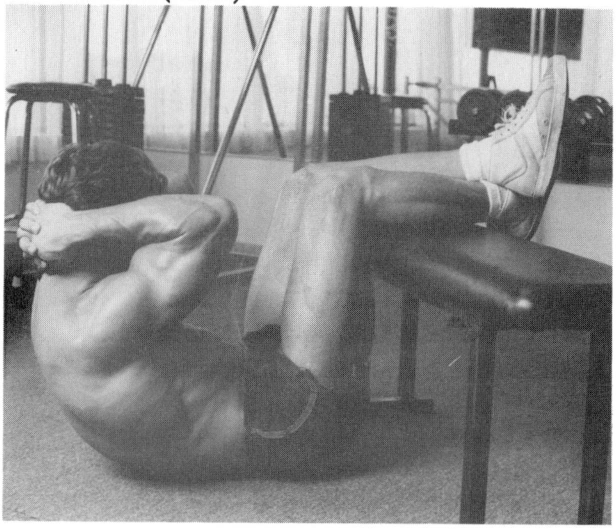

Standing calf raise (start).

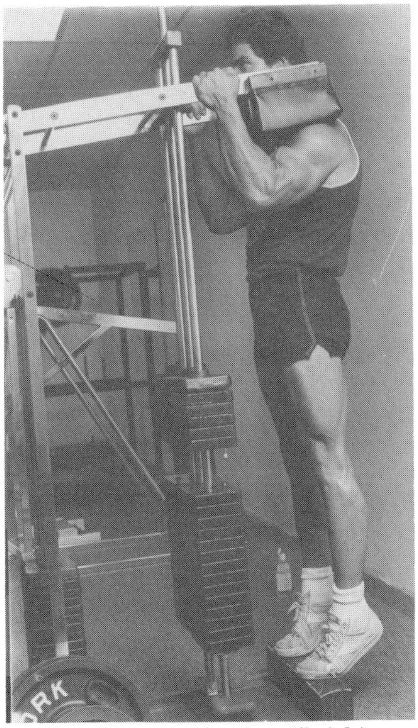

Standing calf raise (finish).

Bench press (start).

Bench press (finish).

Jim Quinn.

CHAPTER 6
NUTRITION AND SUPPLEMENTS

Even today I doubt that most bodybuilders really understand the importance of diet in their training. Most of the people that come to me for advice feel that their progress is 99 percent dependent on their sets and reps and workout frequency, when in fact a good 50 percent of bodybuilding can be attributed to nutritional intake.

There are several aspects to consider with regard to eating for bodybuilding results. The first is the actual quality of the food you ingest. It makes no sense to put inferior foods into your stomach when you are hoping for them to build an outstanding physique. Secondly, the amount of foods you consume is extremely important because you will gain weight if you eat a large amount, and you will lose weight if you eat a small amount. This sounds very simplistic but it's true. The third aspect of food is eating frequency. Whether you are trying to gain weight or lose weight, you must eat small meals frequently throughout the day. This prevents the stomach from being overloaded at any one time, distributes the food nutrients and energy over a more even level, and allows what you eat to be utilized to its fullest by the body's mechanisms.

Remember this: fat is your enemy. True enough, the body needs a certain amount of fat to be healthy. Fat is found in almost all foods that we eat and it is definitely to our advantage to reduce all visible fats as much as possible if we are to build impressive-looking bodies, or if we are to reduce surplus overweight.

As a rule, protein is not a big factor in weight control. Protein feeds the muscles. It is also a fact that after you remove water, the muscles consist mainly of protein. Generally speaking, protein does not affect our body weight in either direction. On the other hand, body fat is affected by the amount of fat we eat. The body is extremely efficient in incorporating dietary fat into its body fat stores. A huge 97 percent of fat calories can be stored on the body around the waist, hips, thighs and lower back, anywhere, in fact, where it will be least disturbed by body motion. The fat reserve will accumulate even if you overeat the tiniest bit of fat. The key to losing weight then, is to eat less fat than your body burns each day. Should you replace fats with carbohydrates, you will benefit doubly, because when you eat complex carbohydrates, vegetables, whole grains, etc., the body has to work harder to get energy and some of the calories are wasted as heat.

Even if you don't want to lose weight I feel very strongly that one should make a concentrated effort to reduce fat in the diet. If you are endeavoring to lose weight because you are carrying too much surplus fat, then try having a lunch of broth-based soups with lentils, rice and vegetables. These contain almost no fat. Tuna, packed in water, for example, has only 1 gram of fat per 85 gram serving. The same product, packed in oil and drained, contains about 7 grams of fat. Bread for use in sandwiches contains 1 gram or so per slice. White meat, chicken, or turkey contain 1 gram of fat per 30 grams of weight. Sliced marbled beef has 6 grams.

The worst type of lunches you can eat are the fast-food variety, such as cheeseburgers, regular fries, and battered fried chicken. There are huge amounts of fats in these typical fast-food lunches. It's interesting to note that most varieties of white fish only have about 1 gram of fat per 115 grams. This makes them an ideal food for those interested in keeping a low body-fat percentage all year round. Rice is the bodybuilder's favorite food. There is no doubt that this product helps greatly in keeping the body functioning well and feeding the muscles in a natural way. Rice can be considered one of the most perfect foods on this planet. Never doubt for a minute that you are what you eat. Go for the best foods and you'll feel wonderful. Eat casually without regard for what you're eating and you will never get anywhere in the bodybuilding game.

I'm often asked which are the best weight-gaining foods. The answer is unequivocal. The best weight gain food is milk. All young mammals double or triple their body weight as a result of drinking milk from day one. It is almost perfect because milk contains virtually all the essential nutrients discovered by man in the correct proportions. However, milk does contain a substantial amount of fat, and even a skinny bodybuilder will gain a thick layer of fat under the skin if too much milk is consumed. Certainly, milk doesn't fit in with a diet designed to reduce fat levels. If you are excessively thin, to the extent that you have the abdominals bursting through the skin around your waist, then by all means drink whole milk and even mix in some soft fruits such as bananas, peaches, pears, or strawberries. But, if you have any tendency whatsoever to be fat, then drink only skim milk which has virtually all the fat removed.

If you are inclined to fat in any way I suggest you also keep to skim milk and low-fat yogurt, and other milk products.

Let's start with breakfast. Cottage cheese, for example, can be used, but eat regular cheddar cheese rarely because it's at least 50 percent fat. Eggs should be boiled, fish should be broiled, and meats should be baked or broiled.

Between breakfast and lunch it's a good idea to have a small snack. This should consist of simple foods such as a yogurt and a banana or a wholewheat bread sandwich with a slice of cooked chicken breast. Lunch doesn't have to be big, but it should be substantial and should contain a high protein food of some sort. Again don't overlook the importance of complex carbohydrates. Often a salad made up of mixed vegetables can be very beneficial for the bodybuilder because it supplies all the enzymes and vitamins necessary for a perfectly functioning body. Protein at lunchtime can come from cold slices of meat or even from unsalted nuts, or broiled or poached fish.

For dinner you might like to start with a wholesome vegetable soup, a salad, a half grapefruit, or a shrimp cocktail. This can be followed by a broiled steak, veal chop, liver, chicken or salmon steak. Vegetables can consist of steamed broccoli, cauliflower, carrots, spinach, or any other vegetables that appeal to your taste. If you need a dessert at this time you can eat fresh melon or yogurt or a mixed fruit salad or simply an apple. Again, because I'm recommending that most meals be similar in size and that you cannot overload your stomach, don't feel that you have to have a full-course meal at dinnertime. In fact I would try to make your evening meal more the size of breakfast, substantial but not huge. Far better to eat again around 9 or 10 at night rather than making your 6 o'clock meal one of large portions which will only serve to make you feel tired and listless.

For those of you who want to lose weight, the last thing you should do is count calories. Scientists tell us that the calorie is a unit of energy but the precise calculation of calories in relation to weight gain or weight loss is not acceptable to me. I have seen too many skinny people who eat all day long to know that consuming a large quantity of calories is not a failsafe way to gain weight. Alternatively, I have seen people consuming fewer and fewer calories and still they are not able to significantly reduce weight. Although a calorie is a unit of energy, research suggests that the energy from different nutrients is not treated the same way by the body. It's primarily the calories from fat that cause overweight, not from protein and carbohydrates.

Following are some thoughts on the type of nutrition that will benefit your bodybuilding the most. Breakfast is important and should consist of a substantial amount of food. A topnotch breakfast for example, might start with an orange, followed by 2 boiled or poached eggs, wholewheat toast, natural preserves without sugar, and a glass of skim milk. By breakfast time you probably haven't eaten for 12 hours or so, and if you miss breakfast and go for several more hours before eating, this creates a situation whereby the period of having no substantial food in the stomach is too long to help maximize bodybuilding progress. We need food in our systems every 2 or 3 hours if we are to make maximum progress. Some people prefer a mixture of dried foods, nuts and grains for breakfast. There are several good mixtures in the supermarkets today. Alternatively a bowl of fresh fruit makes a very good start for a day, but be sure to include some protein which is, after all, what the muscles are made of. Whatever you may read elsewhere, bodybuilders do require slightly more protein than other people, so eggs can form a very good basis for breakfast. It is suggested that if you have 6 to 8 eggs, then you should only have 1 or 2 egg yolks. Many top bodybuilders eat 8 to 12 eggs for breakfast but they only eat 1 or 2 yolks. The egg whites contain much of the goodness while the yolk itself is fairly high in fat.

Are you one of those bodybuilders who hates to eat breakfast? Many people feel nauseated when they get up in the morning. Others find that they're just not hungry. People get used to not having breakfast—often a result of being rushed in the morning. I suggest that these people get up earlier and allow their bodies to adjust to being awake, after which they should feel more like eating breakfast. Start with just a piece of toast, and build up over the weeks until you're having something more substantial. Few people will find that they can't tolerate cereal and milk or a bowl of fresh fruit.

An important aspect of bodybuilding nutrition is that of supplements. Today more than ever supplements are important to make maximum progress. Nutrition could be compared to a bank account. By substituting calories for dollars, you start with a given amount in the bank. Eating is like making deposits in that you add to the total in your bank account. Writing a check can be looked upon as exercise (walking, breathing, weight training, running, stair climbing) and subtracted from the amount in the account. When your deposits equal your withdrawals, your balance (body weight) will stay the same. If you spend as many calories as you eat, your body will stay the same. Burn more calories than you consume and your body will start losing weight (muscle and fat). In theory, for example, if you eliminate just one pat of butter from your diet, you will not deposit some 3,780 calories each month. This represents one pound of body weight and about 12 pounds a year. Eliminate two pats of butter per day and you'll lose about ½ pound per week.

This similarity doesn't end here. Just as you have to pay in to your bank account in genuine currency to accrue the long-term benefits, so, too, should you eat genuine foods to build up a healthy, dynamic well-built physique. Synthetic foods may seem okay when first deposited but like a bounced check, the value is temporary, and if you continue to ingest them you'll soon become physically bankrupt.

Of course, this is not to say that everything that passes your lips must be 100 percent good nutrition, but it sure helps if the majority of what we put in our mouths is good, wholesome, natural food. Too many people eat too much junk and this in turn leads to sickness and loss of overall virility, positive health and general well being. Good nutrition doesn't just involve the foods we eat, it also concerns the way in which we prepare our foods for consumption. Generally speaking, one should select foods on a daily basis from the five main food groups known as:

1. The Milk Group (milk, cheese, yogurt)
2. The Meat Group (beef, lamb, pork, poultry, eggs, fish, veal)
3. Vegetable/Fruit Group
4. Bread/Grain group
5. Fats/Oils Group (butter, margarine, salad oil). Usually only small amounts of these.

This chapter is not for the faddist or the health fanatic, but for the male and female bodybuilder who want to learn how to eat and get an impressive physique. On the other hand, part of eating to get strong and well-built involves eating high-quality food which may also be part of the health enthusiast's diet as well. You need to eat well to build a power-packed body. You train hard for your muscles, so don't allow your efforts to be wasted by ignoring the importance of optimum nutrition. Go for the best you can find, and the best you can afford. Often, incidentally, really top-quality food is less expensive than low-quality junk food.

Fast food has become a part of our diet, but let's keep it to as few visits as possible. You just will not build a prize-winning physique by eating hot dogs, pizzas, hamburgers and spaghetti, most of which have high salt (sodium) and only fair to low fibre content. As for drinks like sodas, and other carbonated soft drinks, chances are you'll get more nutrition if you popped a sugar cube in a glass of brown dye and topped it off with rainwater. If you find yourself eating junk food on a daily basis, your body will reflect that fact and you will not reach your ultimate potential.

The body tends to take on the look of what we put inside it. If we eat good, clean food, such as fruits and vegetables and lean meats and fish, and whole grains, then the body will tend to reflect the quality of our nutritional input. On the other hand, if we eat junk foods on a regular basis, then the skin tone and the pockets of fat under the skin will take on an unhealthy appearance. What are these junk products that we shouldn't eat or eat only occasionally? They are either nutritionally bankrupt or full of sodium, sugar, chemicals, preservatives, coloring, dyes, or artificial flavors. Foods to keep away from as much as possible include synthetic or packaged cakes, pies, cookies, artificial cream, doughnuts, puddings, candies, pizza, hot dogs, smoked meats, potato chips, chocolate bars, beer, pretzels, ice creams and ices, jams, soft drinks, salad dressing, dyed meats, bacon, packaged ham, synthetic sausages, sugary breakfast cereals and anything else that comes pre-packaged. Even canned foods are not recommended mainly because they are packaged in a base of coloring preservatives or sugar. In decaffeinated coffee, caffeine is removed from the coffee bean with methylenechloride, a chemical solvent suspected of causing cancer. Steer away from regular consumption of white flour products, sugar-loaded canned fruits and vegetables, gravies, and deep fried foods of all kinds.

I'm sure by now you're wondering just what you can eat! The answer of course is to keep to natural foods as much as possible. I've listed some of the worst—now for the best.

Make up your meals from wholesome unspoiled food, such as 100 percent whole-grain bread (wholewheat or whole rye), and other natural complex carbohydrates. Base your diet on fresh broiled meats and poultry, fish, eggs, unsalted nuts, fresh fruits and vegetables, and salads. Steam your vegetables; do not boil them. Never fry meat or fish or potatoes or anything else. Don't remove the peel from apples, tomatoes, peaches, and so on. Skin contains nutrients that the food itself does not. Be sure to wash your fruit and vegetables thoroughly since they may have been sprayed with harmful pesticides or insecticides. Don't be fooled into thinking that there are some super foods out there, foods that can either give you phenomenal energy and stamina or help growth faster than anything else or foods that will burn up fat faster than other foods. This just isn't the case. There is no such thing as a super food that will work miracles in changing the body or the body's chemistry. We have good diets and supergood diets, but there is no single superdiet that will make your body function better than normal.

Avoid as much as possible overloading the system with fat, salt and sugar. For example, a typical dinner that might be considered excellent nutritionally is half a grapefruit, followed by a fresh green salad, baked free-range poultry, a baked potato, lightly steamed vegetables and a fresh fruit salad.

Some people take in huge amounts of protein in the belief that their muscles will grow faster than ever. This is a mistake because excessive protein can be stored as fat, and will not necessarily make your muscles bigger; rather, it may well end up around your waist as a spare tire of fat. A gram of protein has 4 calories, the same amount of calories as a gram of carbohydrates (a gram of fat has 9 and a gram of alcohol has 7 calories). There are actually two types of proteins—complete proteins and incomplete proteins. Complete proteins are found mainly in foods of animal origin such as meats, poultry, seafoods, eggs, milk, and cheese, etc. Complete protein provides a proper balance of the nine essential amino acids that build tissues. Incomplete proteins such as are found in seeds, nuts, peas, grains, and beans lack certain essential amino acids, and are not used efficiently when eaten alone. However, when they're combined with even small amounts of animal protein, they become complete in themselves and are as good as any other type of protein.

SUPPLEMENTS

The universal question in bodybuilding is "How do I get bigger as fast as possible without getting fat? I just want to build a large amount of muscle size." Well, don't we all! Gaining muscle without fat is a very real problem with most intermediate and advanced bodybuilders. Supplements: Are they necessary? No, they're not necessary, if you are eating a balanced diet. The bodybuilder, however, is in a different category entirely. You need to gain muscular bodyweight in a healthy and expeditious manner, and often supplements are helpful in doing this. Remember that supplements are not magic. They are *not drugs*; they're merely concentrated foods. There's no reason to believe that the supplement is nutritionally better than the foods from which they are made. In other words, if you eat eggs and chicken, theoretically you would not need a protein supplement to help muscle growth. On the other hand, there is a convenience factor associated with taking a protein powder, mixing it with milk as an in-between snack to feed the muscles.

As far as vitamins and minerals are concerned, no bodybuilder who is eating well needs them. I do believe, however, that a person dieting down for a contest or for a photo session or for any other reason, could well benefit from taking a one-a-day vitamin/mineral tablet. This will ensure that however strict their diet, they will be getting all the minute nutrients found in this type of supplement. It's your assurance that you are not putting your body into a negative balance.

There is a large variance in the amount of protein we require. It depends on a variety of factors including our health, age, sex, size, height, and training habits. Actually the larger and younger you are, the more protein you will need. To estimate your own personal daily recommended allowance see the chart below.

Age	Pound Key
11–14	0.45
15–18	0.40
19 and over	0.36

Find the pound key under your age group, and multiply that figure by your weight. The result will be your daily requirement of protein in grams. For example, if you're 29 years old, and weigh 150 pounds, your pound key is 0.36: $150 \times 0.36 = 54$ grams, which is your daily protein requirement. Most people need at least 45 grams of protein daily. Naturally, if you're keen to build up solid weight, bear in mind that it is always good to be over your minimum daily requirements rather than under. Also take into account the fact that the body can only assimilate approximately 25 grams of protein at any one time. If you take in considerably more than this, much of it will be passed out of the system as waste, and will not be utilized by your body. Or, worse, it will be added to your fat stores.

Should you take in less protein than you require, your body will rob the muscles to make sure that it gets enough protein to keep essential mechanisms such as your heart and lungs in good working condition. So it's easy to see that you should ingest adequate amounts of protein to prevent the body from robbing the muscles to meet the needs of the normal functions of living.

You can buy protein in sports stores, nutrition stores, or health food stores. They generally supply about 24 grams of protein per ounce, which is 2 heaping tablespoons. That's about the equivalent protein value of a 3-ounce steak. The best protein powders on the market are usually those called milk and egg protein powders. The egg is the highest quality protein known, and milk is the second highest quality protein, so the combination of the two works very well. Don't make the mistake of thinking that protein is nonfattening, however. Any food that has significant calorie content is potentially fattening.

Muscles are made of protein, so it stands to reason that the muscle that is worked with progressive resistance exercise, and on which a demand has been placed to get bigger, should be fed sufficient protein. What better way to do it than to take supplementation in the form of a pleasant-tasting shake? A typical way of mixing a protein powder would be to pour some skim milk into a pitcher (making sure the milk goes in *before* any powder goes in), and follow that with 5 or 6 heaping tablespoons of protein. Then you can add soft fruits such as bananas. Some people break a couple of raw eggs in, but that's not my own personal choice. And you can add any other type of flavoring that you feel will make the end result taste better. Some people use chocolate, others prefer strawberries, raspberries, or peaches. The best time to take your protein shake is between supper and bedtime. It will act as a protein snack and feed the muscles while you sleep. If you're trying to gain muscular body weight, you may want to take more than one protein drink a day, but always take it between meals, at a time when it would be most beneficial. Remember, the body can only assimilate 25 grams of protein or so at any one sitting. Protein drinks should be blended in a blender rather than just stirred, because protein doesn't mix easily with liquid.

Many bodybuilders place great importance on what has become known as "steroid substitutes." Ever since it was discovered that

John Terilli.

steroids were used by strength athletes, weightlifters, bodybuilders, and even runners, a wide variety of so-called "steroid substitutes" have come on the market. In actual fact, none of these substitutes work like steroids, but some are better than others. Many bodybuilders take glandulars which are tablets made up of desiccated liver, or kidney or heart. These are merely concentrated protein foods which usually contain about 35 to 40 percent protein. They are utilized by the body and they keep a high protein supply in the bloodstream, so many bodybuilders find there is a benefit in snacking on these between meals or even during meals.

Other so-called steroid substitutes are the various compounds of amino acids. These are marketed in ever-increasing variety, and no one that I know has figured out exactly what does what or what, if anything, is done at all. Amino acids have built the reputation, however, of being in their free-form variety a fairly good substitute for regular protein meals. Amino acids go straight into the bloodstream, and they are used extensively by all competitive bodybuilders that I know. There is also evidence to show that amino acids contribute to gains in size, gains in strength, and gains in loss of body fat. However, my own observation is that amino acids are expensive and the return that they give for the dollar spent is minimal. I have noticed that bodybuilders, whether they're on steroid substitutes or not, do tend to supplement with amino acids more than any other supplement known.

RATING THE SUPPLEMENTS

Our bodies are walking, talking, chemical factories. At any one time, millions of chemical reactions are taking place under our skin, and it is *only* our skin that stops us leaking out thousands of complex chemicals. Many people ask how they can accelerate their bodybuilding progress, and whether or not they should be taking any or all of the various supplements offered in the bodybuilding journals. One thing's for sure, you should never consider taking *all* of them. It may be a good idea, however, to take a few selective items to help you progress towards your goals. Beginner, intermediate and advanced bodybuilders regularly take supplements. There is no doubt that much of what they take is wasted and excreted out of the system.

The purpose of this section is to sort through the facts, fallacies, and fads of bodybuilding supplements so that you can decide for yourself. I've listed most of the popular supplements available today and have put a rating based on the sum total of the following variables: scientific research data, firsthand testimony, price of the supplement relative to its effectiveness, level of necessity in a bodybuilding regimen, and possible placebo effect. Bear in mind, however, that each variable can greatly differ from one person to another. Although we are basically similar in our chemical construction, some people do react to the smallest of things, real or imagined, while others need to be hit over the head in order to be aware something's working for them.

This is a subjective perspective, not a precise scientific analysis.

Five-Star Rating

★★★★★ This signifies that this product is an absolutely excellent item that really should be utilized for your bodybuilding progress.

Four-Star Rating

★★★★ A very good product that has proven value as a bodybuilding supplement, but for some reason, is not as absolutely necessary as is the five-star-rated product.

Three-Star Rating

★★★ A good product but enough doubt exists to cause debate over its ultimate value. The three-star rated product may be valuable to some, while others pass on it for lack of effectiveness.

Two-Star Rating

★★ This signifies that a product is questionable in value but may exhibit a small benefit, either physical or psychological.

One-Star Rating

★ This is a product that science has pretty well discounted entirely. A one-star rated product is more than likely a total waste of money.

I have avoided mentioning brand names because each company feels that its product is absolutely the best there is; it invites argument if I mention actual names. Apart from that, a *poor* brand-name product could change the content of their ingredients and make it a *worthwhile* product, while still keeping their brand name. I am therefore keeping my comments to a generic mode in order to be fair to all concerned. Each nutritional supplement listed is commented on, assuming that it is the highest quality and not something that has been watered down or reduced in concentration.

PRODUCT	RATING	COMMENT
Carnitine	★★★	This product has been shown to be responsible for transporting cellular fat which research indicates could speed up the fat-burning process and help sustain energy during periods of dieting where the calorie intake is considerably lowered. Many professional bodybuilders swear that they can feel it work and others feel that it doesn't have much use. At the present time, little scientific evidence shows that it is effective; however there are a substantial number of experienced bodybuilders who strongly feel it is a worthwhile supplement. Since it is very expensive, if you can't afford this ingredient, you could get a similar effect by performing aerobics such as stationary bike riding.
Dimethyglycine (DMG)	★★★	This supplement is considered useful to those who take their training to exhaustion. DMG is for those who run out of gas during a workout. DMG delays the onset of this drop-off in energy because it reduces lactic acid and increases the efficiency of your oxygen use during heavy sets of exercise. As do many supplements, DMG can be said to work for short cycles, but many bodybuilders swear that its effectiveness wears off with continued use, so use it as a cycle rather than a regular year-in, year-out supplement.
Inosine	★★★★	Most bodybuilders feel that they really do notice a strong help when they take this ingredient because of its unique ability to increase ATP production. This enhances oxygen transport throughout the system, and your workload efficiency is improved. Its downfall is that it can increase uric acid synthesis and therefore you may notice some aches in the joints. So again, like the previously mentioned supplement, it's best to cycle its use.
Tyridoxine-Alpha-Ketoglutirate (PAK)	★★★	This supplement has been scientifically proven to be valuable for those involved in both aerobic or anaerobic activity. It gives more energy to the cells and can also cut down on lactic acid production. Scientifically, it is considered a very useful product, but as yet not too many bodybuilders have gotten too excited over it.
Lipotropics	★★★	This group of vitamins consists of methionine, choline, inositol, and Betaine. This supplement was extremely popular in the late 50's and early 60's. It was used extensively by bodybuilders to decrease subcutaneous fat and was especially lauded by (double Mr. Olympia) Larry Scott in his heyday. This product is not worth taking unless you are involving yourself in a strict diet to reduce body fat. At that time I believe that the taking of lipotropics can help give you a slight edge by emulsifying fat under the skin.

PRODUCT	RATING	COMMENT
Vitamin C	★★★★★	This vitamin is the ultimate preventative maintenance supplement. There is no doubt that vitamin C is one of the most useful vitamins because it aids the bodybuilder in so many ways. It helps preserve the immune system. It helps mend the cells. There is no doubt that it also has some use in warding off heavy colds and the flu. It also helps those of us who bruise easily or hold subcutaneous water before a contest. There is additional evidence to show that vitamin C is one of the best supplements for helping us recover from heavy workouts. Many entire books have been written on the benefits of vitamin C alone. Even though we get the RDA (Recommended Daily Allowance) of vitamin C by following a normal diet, it is suggested that you supplement with additional vitamin C because of the enormous benefits in aiding recuperation, building and strengthening the muscles, and generally helping the bodybuilder.
Digestive Enzymes	★★★★	The food we eat has to be broken down by the digestive system and is therefore absorbed into the body to feed the muscles. It goes without saying that without this process taking place, whatever we may eat is wasted if it isn't fully utilized to help build mass and strength. Digestive enzymes are available at health food stores, and definitely give you a better chance to fully utilize your nutritional intake if they are taken regularly. True enough, many genetically advantaged bodybuilders also have superior absorption, but if there's any doubt about your ability to digest the usually larger quantities of food needed by a bodybuilder, then take these digestive enzymes because they will break down the various foods quicker and enhance your absorption of them, so that they are more fully utilized.
B-6	★★★★	This should definitely be regarded as a bodybuilder's vitamin because a regular ingestion of B-6 will help you utilize your protein foods more efficiently. There is even evidence to show that fat and carbohydrate metabolization is increased when this supplement is taken with meals.
Gamma Oryzanol	★★	This relatively new discovery was introduced to the bodybuilding world in a big way, and it is supposed to increase energy levels and overall stamina. There are no viable claims with regard to this product helping build muscle mass. There have been various scientific studies made of gamma oryzanol and some conclusions have been drawn as to its being effective in repairing tissue; however, as far as bodybuilders are concerned this product has not produced significant increases in energy levels or stamina at the present time.

PRODUCT	RATING	COMMENT
Arginine-Ornithine	★★★	When Sandy Shaw and Durk Pearson first came out with their studies on the use of these ingredients to increase the secretion of growth hormone the study was quickly capitalized on by numerous supplement companies, who came out with arginine and ornithine products, claiming, in many cases, them to be steroid substitutes. The truth is the amounts of growth hormone that these ingredients may coax you to secrete is extremely minute. As far as hoping for an increase in muscle mass as a result of taking these substances, it is very unlikely you would notice the difference. Bodybuilders however, have noticed that their muscle pump is enhanced when they are taking ornithine and arginine, so there appears to be some value even though it is minimal.
Smilax	★	This product came and went extremely fast because, although there are some proponents of its use who claim that it increases testosterone levels, the vast majority of scientific data shows that testosterone levels, if increased at all, are only increased at a very minute level. Smilax is a plant sterol and, according to bodybuilding nutrition expert Gunnar Sikk, our bodies cannot even begin to use it efficiently.
Glandulars	★★★	As indicated before, these can be very useful for a bodybuilder because they form about 38 to 40 percent of desiccated liver, kidney, heart, or whatever glands they're made from. One has to be careful not to take too many at any one time because they can upset the stomach. Take glandulars with meals and don't expect magic results because they only contain high-quality protein, which will serve to feed the muscles, but they do not work any better than a boiled egg or a piece of regular beef. Vince Gironda was the first to inform us that glandulars were a very useful supplement, and Vince used to demonstrate the usefulness by quoting an experiment involving rats put in water. According to the scientific findings those rats fed on glandulars were able to keep swimming far longer than those who were not given glandular supplements.
Soya-Based Protein Powders	★	This protein powder is still being sold simply because it is extremely cheap to produce. Since it's a vegetable protein, it lacks essential amino acids to make it a viable muscle-building ingredient. The biological value is very low unless it is mixed with a milk and egg protein or liquid milk or some essential animal protein which will provide the missing essential amino acids.

PRODUCT	RATING	COMMENT
Free-Form Amino Acids	★★★	This is probably the most taken of all supplements at the present time. Most bodybuilders, as I said earlier on, take free-form amino acids, and most swear by their ability to enhance the appearance of the muscles. Free-form amino acids are expensive so, therefore, unless you are very wealthy, don't take them all year round. It is my opinion, however, that they should be taken for three months prior to a contest, a photo session, or a guest appearance. There is enough evidence to show that free-form amino acids do help us gain an edge when it comes to muscle size, strength and hardness.
Milk and Egg Protein Powders	★★★★	As mentioned before, milk and eggs are the two highest-quality proteins known. Therefore, when we mix the milk and egg protein powder with milk we are creating a pretty dynamic muscle food. Larry Scott used to swear by this, and he popularized this form of protein because it was considered that he was less than genetically gifted as a bodybuilder and the milk and egg product was given the credit for building his 20-inch arms. Larry used to say that he would take at least 6 to 8 tablespoons in a serving rather than the small amounts which were commonly used by other bodybuilders. His reasoning was that in order to grow big one had to eat big. Protein drinks can be made with milk, and fruit, such as bananas, peaches, strawberries can be added. This product is generally considered more cost effective than amino acids.
Mega Packs (vitamin/mineral)	★★★	Few bodybuilders on weight-gaining programs who eat a nutritionally sound diet will need any type of vitamin supplementation. The government has set a recommended daily allowance for most vitamins and all the medical studies and scientific experiments show that those of us who eat a normal balanced diet do not need additional vitamins. There is, however, some doubt as to the importance of vitamins to those of us who are following a calorie-reduced diet. At such a time it is my opinion that you would benefit by taking a mega pack a day of a good brand name to ensure that you are not trying to train your body while actually ingesting less than your minimum daily requirement of vitamins and minerals. I'm not saying that a hard-training bodybuilder shouldn't take these vitamin/mineral mega packs, it's just that it's highly likely that the money will be wasted. True enough, you will be confident in knowing that you are definitely getting all the requirements you need, but there is a ton of evidence to show that you would already be getting sufficient quantities to maintain normal health and well-being.

PRODUCT	RATING	COMMENT
Carbohydrate Powders (metabolic optimizers)	★★★★	This product has been touted heavily in recent years and its main purpose is to help maintain energy levels over an extended period of time. In other words, it is designed to help you keep getting your best from your workouts, at a time when you may normally run out of gas. The formulas vary between the different companies pushing this product, but most bodybuilders don't seem to be able to tell the difference between one product and another. It appears to come down to personal preference.
Chromium Picolinate	★★★	I have no first-hand experience with this supplement and can only quote the results of two studies conducted by Gary Evans, a chemistry professor at Bemidji State University at Bemidji, Minnesota. Both studies showed that the compound "bulked-up" muscle and cut down body-fat percentages. In one study, football players on the same exercise program took either chromium picolinate or a placebo. Those taking chromium picolinate showed an average of 42 percent greater growth in lean body mass and a 22 percent drop in total body fat compared to 1.06 percent drop for the control group. It may be too early to tell but chromium picolinate may be the nearest substitute for anabolic steroids thus far. There is also evidence that this supplement can reduce cholesterol levels in the blood. There are no known adverse side effects of chromium picolinate as yet.

Intensity and concentration make Tony Emmott's sets top quality.

François Muse.

CHAPTER 7
ARMS

BICEPS

The most effective exercise for building the biceps are curls, either with dumbbells or barbells and undergrip chins. The biceps are also strongly influenced by movements such as upright rowing, lat machine pulldowns and all forms of pulley or barbell rowing.

There are numerous gadgets on the market designed to help bodybuilders build bigger biceps.

One such gadget is the arm blaster, a support which hangs around the neck, on which the elbows and upper arms are rested in such a way they are held in the vertical position while you curl with a barbell or dumbbell. You could call the arm blaster the poor man's Scott bench. The Scott, or preacher, bench is probably superior because it can be adjusted in height and at the angle in which it supports the arms. Some Scott benches have angles that vary from about 35° to a full 90° (vertical) angle. This means that you can curl with the upper arms held in place with pulleys or with barbells and dumbbells so that the stress is thrown almost entirely on the biceps itself. Are the preacher bench and arm blasters necessary for building size? No. Many a 20-inch arm has been built without the use of these items. What is offered with this type of apparatus is *added variety* in training. One can keep the biceps guessing by continually chopping and changing exercises, and this is one of the ways to keep the muscles growing.

The preacher bench was first popularized by gym owner Vince Gironda, and he found that it was the most workable biceps exercise for him. It might be interesting to note that if you use a shallow angle, say 35°, on the preacher bench, you will work the lower biceps more severely than any other region. Alternatively, if you set the bench at a 90° angle, then more stretch will be thrown on the center of the biceps. It is generally conceded that 90° angle is best for helping along the development of biceps peak. Don't get the impression, however, that you can significantly lengthen a biceps by performing shallow preacher-bench curls. It just doesn't happen that way. True enough, you will be working the lower part of the biceps, and no doubt it will be the sorest part of the muscle the day after your workout, but even so there will not be a great change in biceps shape as a result of using certain exercises. One simply cannot "pull down" a biceps and make it lower. What can happen is that with a great deal of effort and with concentrated onslaught of exercise for the lower biceps one will create a *slight* alteration in shape. But the ratio of effort to the result is extremely high and verging on the impractical.

What is the most favored biceps exercise? It used to be the two-handed barbell curl which was considered a bulk building biceps exercise. Many champions swore by it in the 60's and 70's. However, today, I think it's been superseded in popularity by the incline bench dumbbell curl. Very few champions, indeed, do not perform this exercise regularly in their workouts. It was a favorite with Steve Reeves in years gone by, and with Reg Park, and then more recently Tom Platz, Eddie Robinson, Vince Taylor, Robby Robinson, Lee Labrada, Samir Bannout, and a host of modern bodybuilding greats.

Talking of Tom Platz, he has a unique way of using the incline bench dumbbell curl that really isn't duplicated by any other bodybuilder. Platz will start by curling a dumbbell, keeping his hips right back into the bench, and his head back against a bench top. When he cannot perform another rep in his strict style, he will then raise his hips from the bench so that he's just supported by his shoulders, and in this position he is able to cheat up the dumbbells for several more gruelling repetitions. When he can no longer perform any more of these cheat reps he will swing the dumbbells into position and lower them slowly, feeling the stress all the way down as the arms straighten. Naturally enough, there comes a time when he cannot even move the dumbbells at all. Does he finish the set? No way. Platz continues on with the same dumbbells, trying to lift them even if he can only move them half an inch or so. Sometimes people who watch him in the gym leaning back on the bench groaning, while nothing appears to be moving, are somewhat confused over exactly what Platz is trying to accomplish. Of course, this is his way of keeping the muscles involved for as long as possible, thereby increasing the intensity and breaking down as many muscle cells in the biceps as is humanly possible. In fact, when he cannot even get one-quarter inch of movement out of his incline dumbbell curls, Platz is still not finished with the set. His final hurrah! is to sit up off the bench, in the seated curling position and to literally throw up the dumbbells, lowering them as slowly as possible for 6 or more wildly cheating repetitions. I don't suggest that you try and follow this excessively intense form of training. I simply offer Platz's method for your mental consumption. It is known that Platz is, when he's in heavy training, one of the hardest exercising humans on earth.

The Incline Dumbbell Curl

Lie back on an incline bench slanted at about 45°. Hold two dumbbells in the arms-down position. It does not matter whether you start the movement with your palms facing in or up. The only difference is that the forearms are brought more into play when the palms are facing in.

Keep your head back on the bench, and simultaneously curl up both dumbbells. Your seat should not come up from the bench at any time during the curl. This will "aid" the biceps in getting the weight up, but in doing so will relieve them of some of the work. If they do less work, then how can they build up size or strength?

As soon as the dumbbells reach shoulder level, lower and repeat. Some bodybuilders actually tense their biceps at the end of the curl when the dumbbells are at shoulder level. It is just another way of maximizing intensity, and whether you choose to do it is up to you.

Brad Verret starts the incline dumbbell curl (below).

The finish

Lying Dumbbell Curl

This is performed in the same way as the incline dumbbell curl, except the bench is completely flat. Most people of average height or taller will have to have a comparatively high bench, so that the dumbbells do not hit the floor at the bottom of the curl.

You may also find that this exercise puts too much stress on your arms because of the unusual position. For this reason, it is advised that you start this exercise with comparatively light weights.

Rich Gaspari uses the E-Z curl bar for his standing curls.

1

2

3

Barbell Curl

Generally considered the king of the biceps builders, the regular barbell curl has contributed to more 20-inch arms than any other movement. If your grip feels awkward, you can use the more comfortable E-Z curl bar.

Hold the bar slightly wider than shoulder width, and keeping your elbows close to your body, curl the weight upwards until it is under your chin.

There are two distinct ways of doing this exercise. You may perform it strictly (no leaning back during the movement, starting from a straight-arm position, utilizing absolutely no body motion or "swing") or by cheating, which involves hoisting the weight up by turning the trunk of your body into a pendulum on which the barbell can rely for added momentum.

Both are workable methods, but most successful bodybuilders find they get best results from doing at least the first 6 or 8 repetitions in strict style and then finishing off the harder last 3 or 4 repetitions with a cheating motion.

Vince Gironda has his own way of performing barbell curls which he calls the body-drag curl. Basically, you hold the bar with a slightly wider grip than normal and lift the bar upwards (dragging against the body) instead of curling it outwards away from the torso. When you have lifted the bar as high as possible, lower it and repeat.

Alternate Dumbbell Curl

This exercise is a great favorite of champion bodybuilder Rocky DeFerro. Unlike the two-handed dumbbell curl, this movement works the biceps more directly in that the exercise prevents undue leanback or cheating. Perform the movement by standing erect. First curl one dumbbell, and then, as it is lowered, curl the other arm. Lower slowly and do not swing the bells up with any added body motion.

Laura Creavalle enjoys the alternate dumbbell curl.

Nautilus curls: Mike Mentzer works on the apparatus.

Nautilus Curls

Place your hands carefully in position under the Nautilus pads and clench your fists. Do not begin the movement with a jerk but rather commence with a slow, deliberate, totally motivated commitment to curl both arms together. Lower and repeat. According to Arthur Jones, the creator of Nautilus, 1 set of maximum reps is sufficient, but that 1 set must contain total effort. Today, most bodybuilders feel that a minimum of 3 sets is required for maximum effect.

Single-Arm 45° Pulley Curls

A super finishing biceps exercise. Mr. America Tim Belknap will attest to the pumping effect of this movement. Curl the pulley apparatus smoothly and deliberately, concentrating all the time on the biceps muscle itself. If you choose to finish your biceps routine with this movement, you may perform anything from 15 to 20 reps. The pump will be unbelievable.

Tonya Knight performs the single-arm 45° pulley curl.

Seated Dumbbell Curl

Sit on the end of a bench with your knees together and back straight.

Starting from the arms-hanging position, begin to curl both dumbbells simultaneously, lower, and repeat. If you have difficulty curling the weights without leaning backwards, it is a good idea to have a training partner place his foot on the bench, positioning his knee in the middle of your back. Alternatively, he can sit on the bench with his back against your back. Both positions will prevent you from excessive leaning back.

If you don't have a training partner, alternately lift the dumbbells one at a time.

François Muse begins the seated dumbbell curl (above) and finishes (right).

Larry Scott at age 50 performs the steep angle Scott curl.

Steep Angle Scott Curls

Set the bench at 80° to 90°, making sure that the bench is adequately padded so that it fits comfortably under your armpits, and affords maximum comfort for the elbows. This is important because you need to be able to concentrate fully on an exercise, and if you are in pain because of inadequate padding, you will not be able to give the exercise your entire mind.

Always start each repetition with the arms straight. Under no circumstances, "bounce" the weight up. This bad habit has caused many torn biceps muscles, some so severe as to have required surgical repair.

This is a favorite of Mike Mentzer's and was popularized by Larry Scott (hence the name). Previously, it was known as the preacher curl or the Gironda curl since its greatest and earliest popularity came about from Vince Gironda.

Concentration Curl

Sit at the end of a bench resting your elbow on the inside of the thigh (above the knee). Exercise only one arm at a time, resting the nonexercising hand on your free leg.

Slowly curl the straight arm upwards and lower at the same speed. Concentrate dramatically on the biceps muscle as it contracts each time the dumbbell is curled upwards. After training one arm, immediately do an identical number of repetitions with the other one.

Arnold Schwarzenegger has another version of this curl which he feels has contributed more to his monumental biceps size and peak than any other. He places one hand on a low stool or exercise bench and holds a dumbbell at arm's length hanging downwards. Arnold makes a point of keeping his shoulder low throughout this exercise. This movement which Arnold favors does in fact "hit" the biceps in an unusual fashion. It may take you a few workouts to get the hang of it, but once you do, I am sure you will benefit enormously.

Of the hundreds of other exercises for the biceps, the above are, in my opinion, the best.

There has been much discussion about the act of twisting (supinating) the hand as a dumbbell is curled upwards. Arnold Schwarzenegger was one of the first people to popularize the theory that this action, as a movement dependent upon the biceps, would contribute to added biceps height. Arnold really believed that twisting the wrist as the dumbbell curl was completed would help his biceps development. What he neglected to conclude was that the simple act of twisting the wrist, even when holding a heavy dumbbell, could not possibly do anything for the biceps, unless, of course, it was done against significant resistance.

Now, if the inner side of the dumbbell was loaded with considerably more weight than the outside, you would have some extra resistance during the supination. Alternatively, if you held the dumbbell unevenly, allowing as much space as possible between your little finger and the weight discs, that too would afford resistance for the twisting and could contribute towards development of the biceps.

There has been a tremendous controversy over whether or not there is such a thing as a biceps exercise that actually helps build height, sometimes known as peak. Again, let me remind you that biceps shape (what we are talking about when we consider degrees of peak) is not something that is receptive to any appreciable change. You can plump up the bundles of fibres within the biceps muscle which will increase the overall size of the area, but there is very little you can do to improve biceps height. The more positive movements include concentration curls, 90° Scott bench curls, and plenty of posing of the biceps themselves, but all in all only minor change will result.

One thing, of course, that does improve biceps peak is to lose every bit of fat possible from the area. You will, no doubt, have noticed that fat people or bodybuilders who have overbulked their bodies do not possess biceps peak. This is because the covering of fat "flattens" out the muscle. An analogy could be drawn with what happens to rugged terrain when it is covered with a generous layer of snow. The entire landscape smooths out. So it is with your arms. The fat fills in between your biceps and your shoulders, and in the crook of your elbows. Voilà! Unimpressive biceps peak!

Arnold Schwarzenegger prefers the standing position when performing the concentration curl.

The concentration curl demonstrated by Ron Love.

TRICEPS

There are probably more exercises that work the triceps than any other body part. This muscle is a three-headed section situated at the back of the upper arm. Of course, it makes sense to work the various sides so that the fullest amount of impressiveness can be built. There are hundreds of triceps exercises. I think it would benefit you to know which are genuinely recognized as being the best triceps builders. Here is my list that I have compiled:

Close Grip Bench Press

Lying Triceps Stretch

Parallel Bar Dips

Pressdowns on Lat Machine

Single Arm Dumbbell Triceps Stretch

2 Arm Single Dumbbell Triceps Stretch

Seated Triceps Rear Bench Dips

Cradle Bench Pulley Extensions (Face Down)

Of course, there are scores of other favorites; some bodybuilders swear by exercise such as close hand floor dips, while others like to perform incline bench dumbbell and barbell movements, and then there are the various machines, like the Cybex or Nautilus machines, that are designed specifically to build triceps. Many of these have a lot of usefulness. Curiously the E-Z curl bar was invented for exercising the biceps muscle. The idea behind it was to make the gripping of the bar more comfortable for both the hands and the angle of the forearms. However, E-Z curl bars are used frequently in the Scott bench curls, but today they are not used too much for standing barbell curls because they do not contribute to working the biceps *more* thoroughly than the straight bar. Ironically, however, the E-Z curl bar is used extensively in triceps work. Most commonly it is used in the close grip bench press, where sweaty hands are likely to edge outwards towards the collars. The curve in the middle of the E-Z curl bar prevents this unwanted movement. Likewise in the overhead triceps extension, the center of the bar is used, and again the curve prevents the hands from working their way out of the central position. There is definitely added comfort in using the E-Z curl bar for virtually all barbell triceps movements and there is no loss in action as there is when one uses an E-Z curl bar for the standing barbell curl.

The triceps itself is a very strong muscle and when fully developed can add enormously to your arm size. Well built triceps can add 5 or more inches to the girth of your arm. One important aspect of triceps building which you might not think to consider unless you personally have suffered it, is an elbow injury. This can occur from three incorrect training procedures, which are:

1. Using too heavy a training load.
2. Bouncing the weight in a clumsy or cheating style.
3. Failing to warm up.

All triceps movements serve to "open up" the elbow in a way that can lead to injury if sufficient warmup is not undertaken. In cases of multi-joint movements like the close grip bench press, or the parallel bar dips, there is probably no reason why heavy weights and low reps cannot be utilized. However, in exercises where a single joint is mobilized such as the triceps pressdown, or the single arm triceps extension overhead it is advised that higher reps only are used. If you try and use heavy weights with low reps in this type of uni-joint exercise you are asking for elbow problems.

Thousands of bodybuilders in their haste and enthusiasm to build 20-inch arms, have injured the delicate tendons surrounding the triceps by trying to use *too* heavy a resistance. The answer is that one must seek to stress the *muscle mass* as opposed to the *elbow joint*. Be content to add poundages in small increments and keep to very strict style in most triceps exercises, and most certainly do not make a habit of performing low reps without adequate prior warmup sets.

Yes, the triceps muscles can handle heavy poundages but the joints cannot follow suit. If you find that a particular triceps exercise is giving you pain while you're performing it, then stop that exercise. Sometimes a simple change of grip will alleviate the problems. For example, in the lying triceps stretch, or the standing triceps pushdowns on the lat machine, simply turning the hands over using the French grip may be all that is needed to take the pressure off the joint and tendon areas. The problem with this is that it's harder to hold onto the bar.

The longer I am in this bodybuilding game the more I'm starting to realize that the triceps are a high rep muscle. That is to say that along with the thighs, calves, forearms and abdominals the triceps do tend to respond well to higher repetitions, and by higher I mean anything from 15 to 50. I'm not saying that most sets should be of these high repetitions (I think most sets should be between 8 and 12 repetitions). However, I do feel strongly that when high repetitions are used in triceps work, that added size will result that one couldn't get from any other form of training.

Old-timer Jack Delinger, a Californian and a past Mr. Universe, who incidentally had the most remarkable triceps of his era, used to insist that when he couldn't get any more size out of his triceps he would double the reps from 10 to 20 for a few weeks and then revert back again to the normal 10 to 12 reps after he had jolted his muscles into new growth.

I also think that the giant set principle works well with triceps exercises, that is, the use of four or five different exercises, performing one right after the other without any significant rest. You can vary the reps while performing this principle too. It's not necessarily wrong to vary reps from 8 all the way up to 30 to 40 or even 50. The idea is to work the triceps from a *variety* of angles and to pump them full of blood so that growth is practically forced upon them.

Who has the best looking arms in the world? With regard to triceps I have never seen better than those triceps displayed by Frank Zane and Mohamed Makkawy. Two semi old-timers, agreed; however, I haven't seen their triceps shape bettered even though I attend 15 to

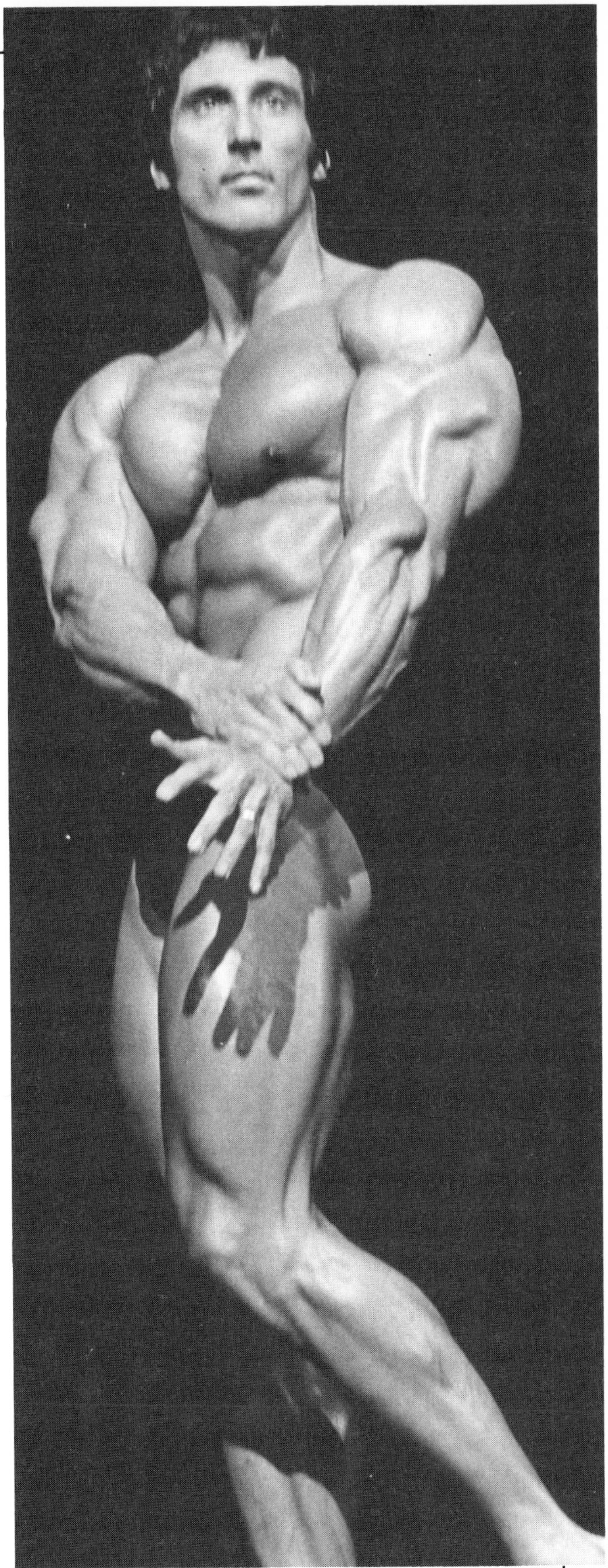

The perfect triceps of Frank Zane.

20 contests a year at this present writing. With regard to biceps, Larry Scott had great biceps, as did Arnold Schwarzenegger, but I think the most amazing biceps I have ever seen belong to Britisher Bertil Fox.

Way back when I was a kid in Art College I joined a bodybuilding club in England run by a bodybuilder named Stan Chisnell. Even though Reg Park was in his prime at that time, Stan was acknowledged as having the largest upper arms in Britain. They measured just over 19 inches around. (Park actually went on to beat this measurement a few years later, becoming one of the few men in the world to possess genuine 20-inch arms.)

I learned a great deal from Stan who combined just two triceps exercises each workout, the Standing Triceps Stretch and the Back Press with Strands. Stan did at least 8 to 10 sets of heavy bench presses each workout and made no bones about the fact that he believed this heavy bench work contributed considerably to his triceps size, as well as his huge pectorals.

Stan would do 5 quality sets of fairly heavy Triceps Stretch movements, using about 10 reps each set, after which he would get his famous rubber cable set out, "toss" the cables over his shoulders with the rubber strands stretched across the back, elbows tucked into his waist. From this position he would press out to "crucifix" position, arms parallel to the ground. Stan would always start light using no more than three or four cables. After each set he would add a cable, until after 5 to 10 sets, the entire group of cables would appear a mass of rubber. Even though there was only room on his set of strands for ten cables, he would somehow find a way to attach more. By the time he was finished, the pump was superb. The cables would go back into his training bag and Stan would mosey off to the washroom, which housed the one and only mirror in the building. Sometimes when Stan felt he had obtained a really outstanding pump, he would invite a few of us skinny guys "to have a little look." We would just stand there, boggle-eyed and open-mouthed as he flexed his ponderous arms from several different angles, murmuring to himself something about "feeling pretty good." Heck, we knew he felt "good." His arms were almost 10 inches bigger than ours!

Out of his storehouse of wisdom, I've never forgotten Stan's insistence on working his triceps *last* in his routine. "Psychologically it's a great feeling," he said, "to end your workout with a really good arm pump." He was so right.

Here's how to perform my recommended triceps movements. Remember not to perform them all in one workout.

Lying Triceps Stretch

Almost every top bodybuilder owes some of his triceps size to this proven exercise. It builds bulk into the belly of the triceps.

Lie on a bench, face up. Using a straight barbell, with a grip slightly wider than the width of the bench, start with arms straight, pointing upwards. Slowly lower the weight by bending at the elbows only. Take the bar down to just behind the head, being careful not to "pin" your hair, until the bar lightly kisses the bench. Do not bounce it heavily. Return the weight to arms-straight position, trying to keep the elbows in at all times. Lower and repeat.

Close-Grip Bench Press

A great favorite of Larry Scott, the first Mr. Olympia, who has said this exercise has given him more triceps development than any other:

Lie on a flat bench, face up, feet firmly planted on the floor. Take a fairly heavy barbell (E-Z curl bars are the most popular among the pros) from the racks (or have a partner hand it to you) using a narrow grip whereby your hands are only 2 or 3 inches part. Keeping your elbows close to your body, lower the weight to your lower breastbone and immediately push upwards. Larry Scott and Dennis Tinerino both use in excess of 250 pounds in this movement, but, naturally, if you are new to this or any other exercise you should start using only light weights.

John Terilli begins the lying triceps stretch (above) and finishes (right).

Dennis Tinerino starts the close-grip bench press (above) and finishes (below).

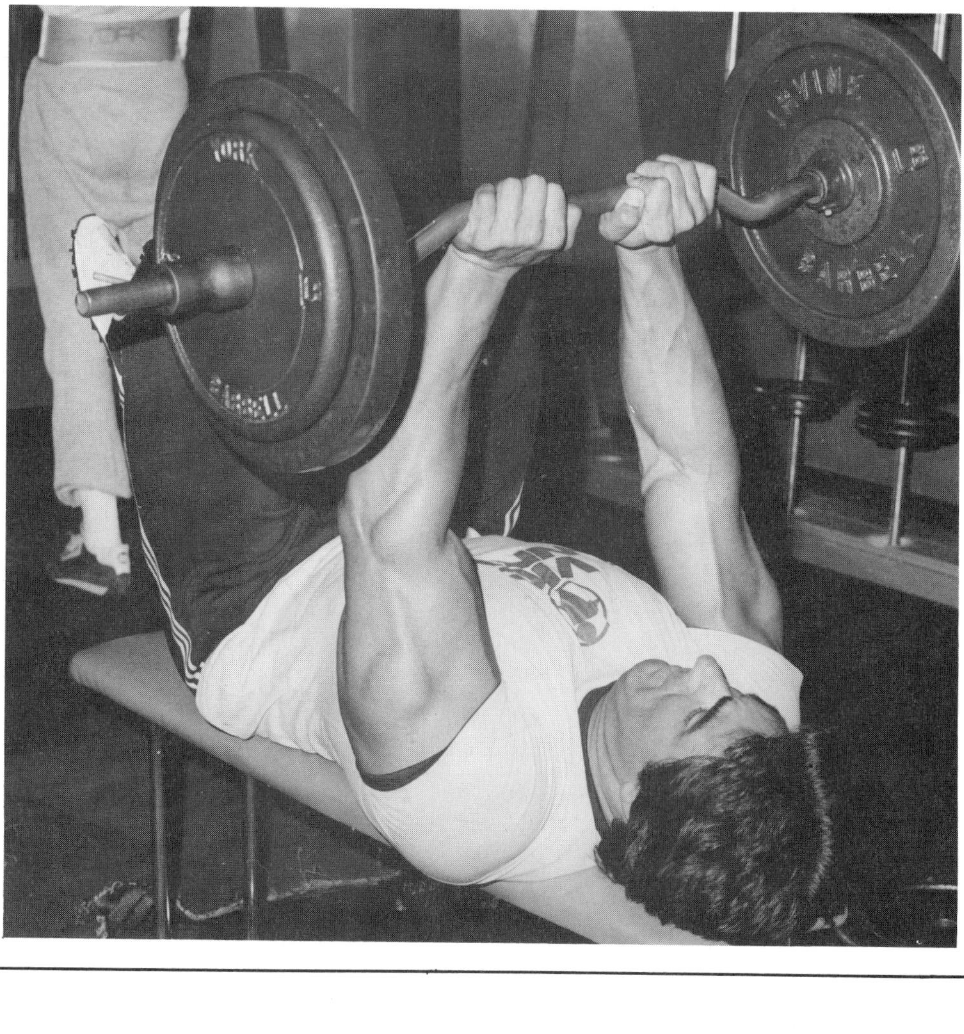

Bertil Fox starts pressdowns on the lat machine.

The finish of the pressdowns on the lat machine.

Pressdowns on Lat Machine

Was there ever a bodybuilder who didn't spend a great deal of time and effort performing this exercise? Bertil Fox loves this exercise.

Start by holding a lat machine bar with hands 2 to 8 inches apart. Now press downwards until the arms are straight. Return and repeat. Most bodybuilders keep their elbows at their sides during this movement. A few (Dennis Tinerino) deliberately hold the elbows out to the sides and "lean" more into the exercise. The choice is yours.

Parallel bar dips are favored by Samir Bannout for triceps development.

Parallel Bar Dips

Samir Bannout endorses this exercise. Start with arms straight, feet tucked up under the torso, and lower (dip) while keeping elbows close to the body. Raise and return. As you get strong enough to perform 10 or 12 repetitions, then weight should be added, either by "holding" a dumbbell between the thighs, crossing feet at the ankle, or by attaching iron discs to a special "dipping belt" designed especially for the task.

Triceps Rear Bench Dips

Numerous bodybuilders, Arnold Schwarzenegger among them, end their triceps workouts with several sets of high repetition rear bench dips. Start by standing with your back to a workout bench, and support the body by resting the hands behind you on the bench, about 6 inches apart. Lift your legs off the floor and support them with a somewhat higher bench. Dip down by bending the elbows as low as possible, and return. You may place a weight disc on your thighs if the movement is too easy. Go for high reps, performing 2 or 3 sets before retiring to the shower room with an almighty pump.

Bent-Over Triceps Extension

Another favorite: Lean over so that the upper body is parallel to the floor. Hold a single light dumbbell in the hand and keeping the upper arm in line with the body (parallel to the floor), raise and lower the dumbbell. Keep the upper arm locked against the side of the waist.

Arnold Schwarzenegger performs triceps rear bench dips.

The bent-over triceps extension shown by Tony Pearson.

John Terilli begins the single-arm dumbbell triceps stretch (above) and finishes (right).

Single-Arm Dumbbell Triceps Stretch

This triceps exercise gives development especially in the lower triceps area. Although it is possible with practice to handle very heavy poundages (some top bodybuilders use over 100-pound dumbbells), it is not always advisable to use excessive weights in this particular movement because they can put too much strain on the elbow joints and the surrounding ligaments. Beware of the movement: This too can cause elbow problems.

A truly great forearm.

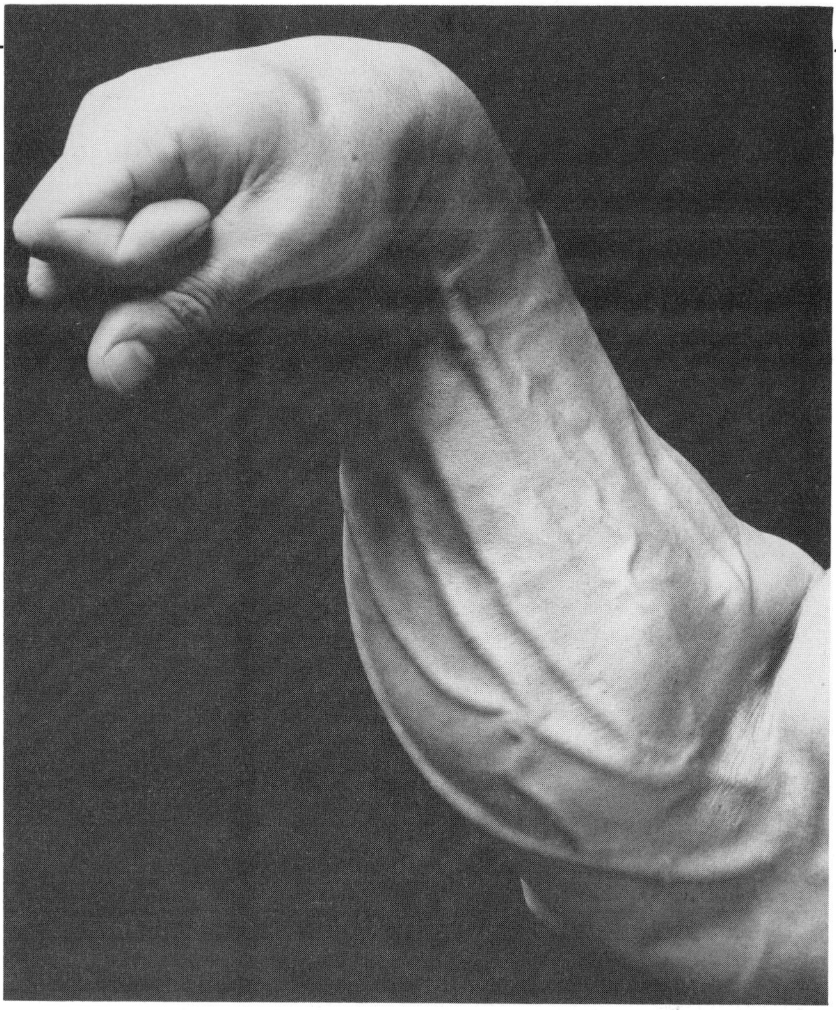

FOREARMS

I used to look at the amazing forearms of Larry Scott, Dave Draper, and Bill Pearl and wonder, "How on earth did they build such enormous lower arms?" It's just too much. Then came Mike Mentzer with equally impressive forearms. But unlike Scott, Draper, and Pearl who trained their forearms regularly, Mr. Mentzer did no specialized forearm training at all. He claimed that his forearms grew from his high intensity workouts. (Mentzer did fewer sets per exercise, but took every set to beyond failure using forced reps and negative reps after he got to the stage in a particular set where another rep was impossible.)

After Mentzer came Tim Belknap who seldom worked his lower arms with special exercises, yet he too had enormous forearms. And today we have stars such as Samir Bannout, Lee LaBrada, Bev Francis and the amazing Steve Brisbois, all of whom have great forearms and only half of whom train them with any regularity. What does this tell us? First, we should understand that virtually every weight training exercise where we hold a barbell or dumbbell involves the forearms. In some genetically advantaged individuals this is enough. The forearms grow from the spillover effect. However, others who may not quite have the cell allocation in the forearms enjoyed by those with superior genetics, may find that they positively *need* to train their lower arms with specialized training.

The forearms usually fall into one of two distinct categories. Some individuals have an "Indian club" type of development which is typified by a long wrist, with virtually no appreciable muscle development except right near the crook of the arm. No amount of exercise will give you a lower forearm or significant development anywhere near the wrist.

Jusup Wilkosz does reverse curls.

The other type of forearm is the "natural" where muscular development begins almost from the base of the thumb. These people's forearms grow from all-round weight training—in fact, the mere act of driving a car can build massive forearms on these lucky individuals.

If you have difficulty in developing your lower arms then make sure that you train them with a couple of the exercises mentioned in this chapter, twice a week. And most important: You must train them progressively, that is, try to add resistance every few workouts, or else increase the number of reps. The forearms, like most muscle areas will only react to the demand of additional stress in the form of heavier weights or more repetitions with the same weight.

Don't be afraid to use higher reps. The forearms are a high-rep muscle. I would never advise using less than 12 reps for your lower arm training, and there's no reason why you shouldn't work up to sets of 20 to 30 reps. The forearms are tough and they need to have blood pumped into them to force them to grow. This is accomplished with higher reps, but also by reducing the rest period between sets. It's a good idea to blitz your forearms occasionally by using supersets, and taking virtually no rest between each set. Your forearms will thank you for it with extra size.

Some people like to carry a hand-grip exerciser or rubber ball in their pockets so that they can squeeze away at odd times during free moments. This may be suitable for tennis players or golfers who need a stronger grip, but serious bodybuilders need more. There are numerous better exercises which work the forearms more fully than a grip exerciser or a rubber ball. Here are a few of them:

Reverse Curl

Stand erect, holding a barbell at a slightly wider than shoulder width. Allow the arms to hang down straight, elbows at your sides, hands overgripped (knuckles up).

Curl the barbell, keeping the wrists straight, elbows tucked in. Lower and repeat. You will feel this exercise in the upper forearm, near the elbow. You may also perform this exercise on a Scott preacher bench.

Power Gripper Machine

This machine is not very common, but it can give the forearms a very thorough workout, and allows for a comprehensive use of progressive resistance to fullest advantage.

One way to build both strength and size into the forearms is to take up nail or spike bending. It is, of course, advisable to start with the light-gauge metals. Blunt them first to avoid accidents, and prewrap the nail by rolling it in a piece of chamois leather. After practice you may be able to do more than bend 6-inch nails—You may be able to *break* them!

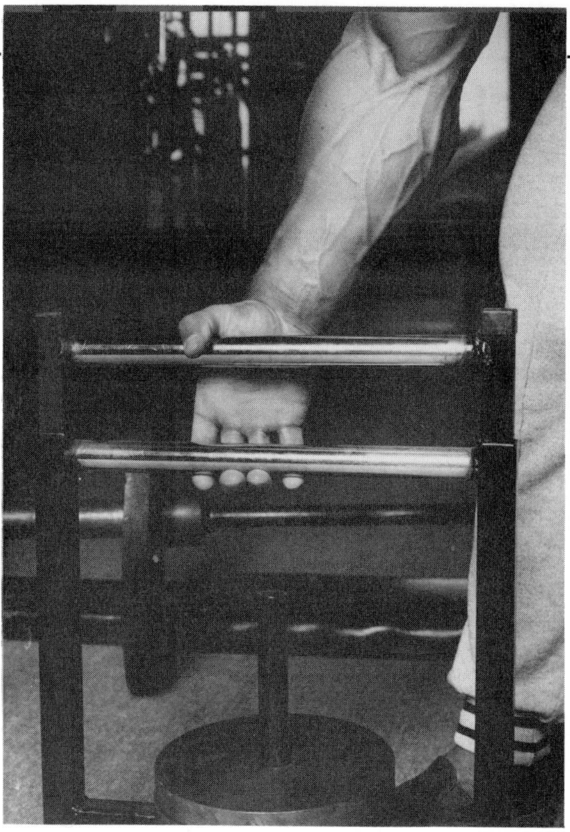

Tim Belknap begins the forearm gripper machine workout (above) and finishes (below).

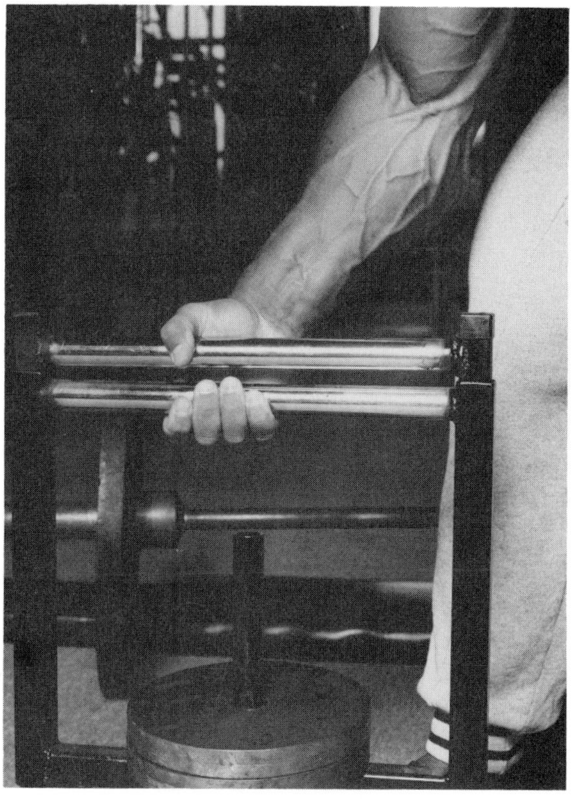

Wrist Curl

Wrist curls work the flexors (the belly) of the forearm.

Perform them in a seated position with your lower arms resting either on your knees (palms up) or on the top of a bench. Your hands must be free. Arnold Schwarzenegger keeps his elbows close while other stars allow their elbows to be comfortably apart (anything from 12 to 18 inches).

Moving only your wrist, curl the weight upwards until your forearm is fully contracted. Allow the barbell to lower under control and (like Schwarzenegger and Draper) you may allow your fingers to "unroll" to an extent, but this is optional.

Reverse Wrist Curl

This exercise is performed in the same manner as the regular wrist curl, the only difference being that the palms should face downwards rather than upwards. You will notice that you cannot use even half as much weight in this reverse wrist curl movement. Most people find it more comfortable to keep the arms at least 12 inches apart in this variation.

Start of the wrist curl as performed by Arnold Schwarzenegger (above) and the finish (below).

Steve Brisbois starts the reverse wrist curl (above) and finishes (right).

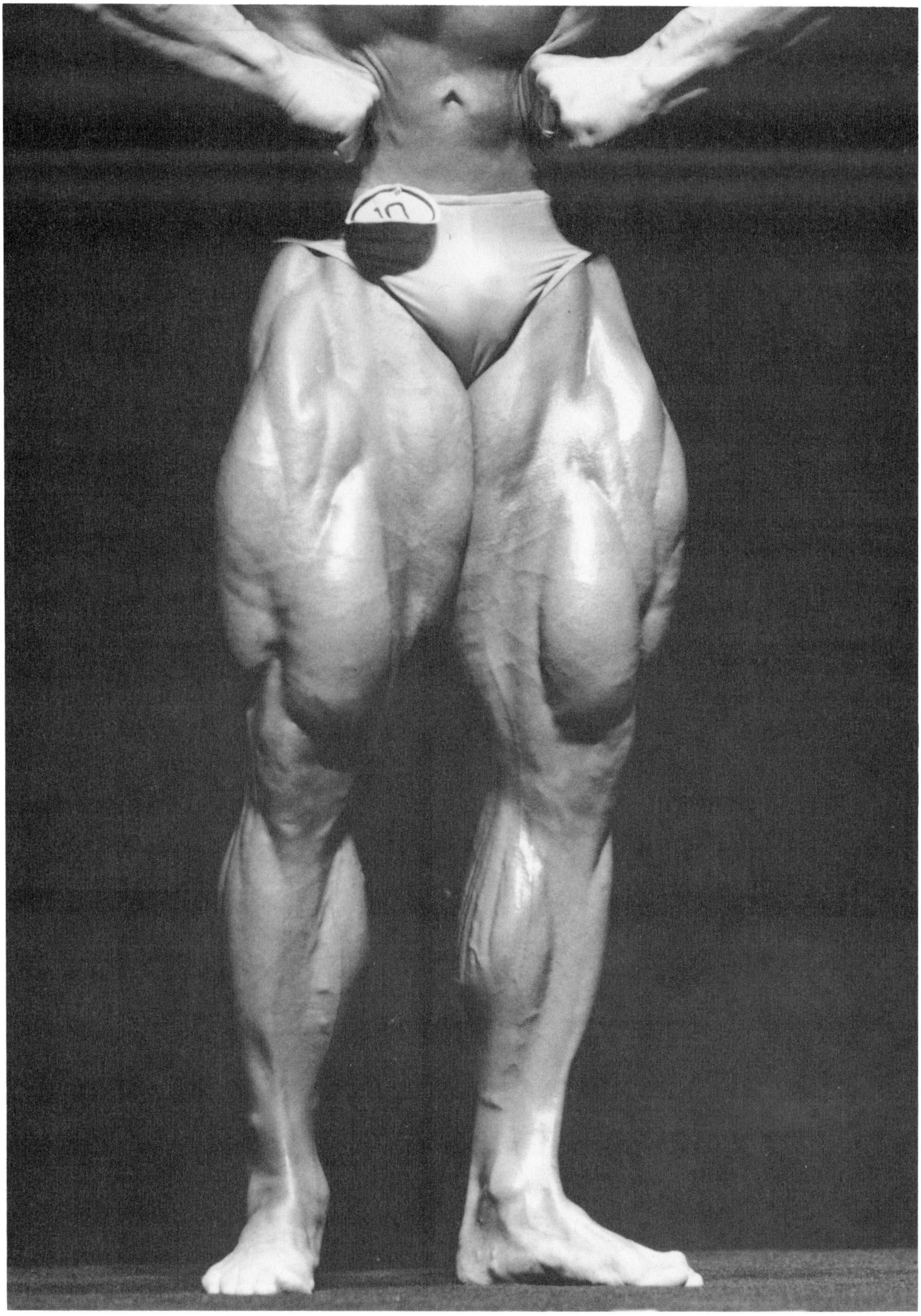

The unmistakable thighs of Tom Platz.

CHAPTER 8
UPPER LEGS

Basic back squats pretty well took care of the upper legs in the 40's, 50's and 60's. But in the 70's things began to change. Bodybuilders looked for ways to enhance upper leg shape and muscular delineation. Of course, back in the 40's there was a handful of bodybuilders who realized the importance of variety in leg training, among them Vince Gironda and Steve Reeves. In fact, neither man believed in going overboard with heavy back squatting, feeling that the upper thighs would overenlarge and the glutes would spread. Their fears were partially true. If you perform back squats and overeat, then there will be a tendency for the upper thighs and hips to spread. However, if your diet is kept under control, then your bodyweight will stay relatively low in bodyfat and the muscles will keep shapely and tight.

Of course, you have to squat correctly, too. Coming out of a deep-knee bend with your head between your knees, butt first, is *not* the proper way to perform this exercise.

Gironda and Reeves and a handful of other ahead-of-their-time bodybuilders preferred hack lifts, thigh extensions, thigh curls and front squats. These exercises kept excessive development away from the hips and upper thighs. More concentration was placed on thigh sweep, leg biceps curve, and overall thigh separation.

In my younger days, I fell into the squatting syndrome. Because I was excessively thin I concentrated on the back squat and ate almost 5,000 calories a day! I gained weight alright, but because of my high-calorie food intake this weight was more bulk than muscle (or even more fat than bulk). And boy did those hips s-p-r-e-a-d.

Gary Strydom's amazing leg musculature.

1. Do not squat while eating excessive calories over and above the body's needs.

2. The squat should be performed correctly (back flat, head up, torso erect, no bouncing).

3. The squat should be used in conjunction with other exercises for the frontal thigh such as leg extensions, hack lifts, lunges, etc.

4. Two-thirds of your upper leg program should be devoted to training the hamstrings (the back of the upper leg). This maintains balance of strength between the opposing muscle groups.

5. If there is any indication of knee problems, do not squat below parallel (where the thighs drop below being parallel to the floor).

Yes, squats are considered the king of all exercises. There is ample evidence to show that squats can release growth hormone into the system, encouraging overall gains in muscular bodyweight. Squatting works the body's biggest muscle groups. This results in increased heart action and deeper breathing. The metabolism is stimulated. More growth results, and not just in the legs. Some experts insist that sets of heavy squatting for 15 to 20 reps actually does more for arm size than triceps extensions and curls.

Squatting is a killer. Let's face it. The movement is extremely uncomfortable. More often than not you run out of air before your thighs give out. The bar grazes your upper spine. Your lungs feel crushed and you may even feel physically sick. Here is how to make your squats more comfortable.

1. Perform them while resting your heels on a 2-inch-high block of wood. (Some people use books.) This will help hold your back upright and prevent you from coming up out of the squat, bottom first, with your head between your knees, a most unwise habit.

2. Lower only until the tops of your thighs are parallel to the floor. Do not squat deeply and on no account bounce out of a low squat position.

Realizing my mistake, I did a 90° turnaround and spent most of my leg workouts performing front squats, hack thigh extensions and leg curls. It helped, but my legs didn't grow.

Today, I have a more balanced view of training. I believe the back squat is an excellent exercise, but the following conditions should apply:

3. Place the bar securely behind your neck and hold onto it tightly, hands about 27 to 30 inches apart. Really skinny people may find that they need to pad the bar (roll a towel around the middle, or use some foam rubber) to prevent it from cutting into the upper back. This habit should be stopped, however, as you develop some muscle. You will soon learn to find a suitable resting position for the bar as you get "into" squatting.

4. If you find that you are gasping for air even before your thighs are giving out, you must develop more cardiovascular efficiency (wind). Run two or three times a week, skip rope, cycle, or swim. Nothing is more uncomfortable than gasping for air with a heavy weight across your back. If you develop good wind, squatting will be far less obnoxious.

5. Always use a good set of squat racks with "catchers." If your racks do not have this safety feature, you need a training partner (preferably two) to spot you during the exercise. This will allow you to concentrate on the task at hand rather than worry that you might get stuck in the squat position.

Today, thigh development forms an important part of bodybuilding competition. Not only are the judges looking for overall size both in the upper, middle, and lower regions of the thigh, but also for well rounded leg biceps. In addition, the sectors—vastus internus and vastus externus—must be fully developed and balanced. The upper thigh must be pronounced, showing all the intricacies of development and separation. Even the abductor muscles must show as should the sartorius on the inner thigh. Cross-striations seen on bodybuilders in top shape are also a plus in any competition.

Who has the best upper legs in the business? Certainly in days gone by Reeves was a top contender. But judging by today's standards Gironda was way ahead of his time. He had upper leg muscularity that went from his knees to his groin. Today bodybuilders like Samir Bannout, Shawn Ray, Lee Haney, Lee LaBrada, Cory Everson, Anja Langer, Tonya Knight and Tony Pearson have complete thighs in that they possess full development and muscular separation right from groin to knee.

A famous bodybuilder once asked me, "Bob, how do guys like Samir Bannout and Tony Pearson get that thigh separation right at the top of the leg where they seem to come out from under the pose trunks?"

The answer is plenty of leg exercises, such as lunges and leg presses, coupled with a low-calorie diet (the thinner the skin the more a muscle will "show"). But most important of all is to "pose out" the area. That is to say, you must constantly practice controlling and posing the upper area of your thighs. Place one foot 6 inches forward and press your heel into the ground, concentrating on bringing out the upper thigh. It is this, more than any other formal exercise, which will give that special look to the upper thigh area. Give it 10 minutes every day and look for real results after a couple of months.

"Mr. Legs" Roger Stewart.

Tonya Knight is spotted in the squat by Marjo Selin.

Squat

It is sometimes known as the basic squat, back squat, regular squat or formal squat; it is surely the superking of all leg exercises.

Take a loaded barbell from the squat racks. After securing it behind the neck, holding the bar in place with the hands, step one step backwards from the racks. Using a block of wood 2½ inches high under the heels, squat down until the upper line of the thighs is parallel to the floor. Return to standing straight position and repeat. During the movement it is necessary to keep the back flat, seat stuck outward, and head up. All squats should be performed either in front of a mirror or a plain wall. This allows for minimal distraction and utmost concentration on what you are doing. It is important to breathe deeply during your squats. Fill the lungs with air before descending and wear a belt during the exercise.

Hack Slides

This exercise is done on a special hack slide machine. Place your feet comfortably apart and slide up and down by bending and straightening your legs. Do not handle too much weight. It is better to perform the exercise with a steady rhythm rather than use a heavy weight that may cause you to fall out of position and work the thighs incorrectly.

Steve Brisbois at the start of the hack slide (above) and at the finish (right).

Thigh Curls

Lie on your front, with your feet about 12 inches apart. Curl up on a thigh curl machine and lower under control. Do not allow the feet to drop, but rather let the thigh biceps *feel* the effort as the weight is lowered. Some thigh-curl machines allow for upright single leg curls, while others are designed to work the hamstrings in the seated position.

Gladys Portugues demonstrates the thigh curl.

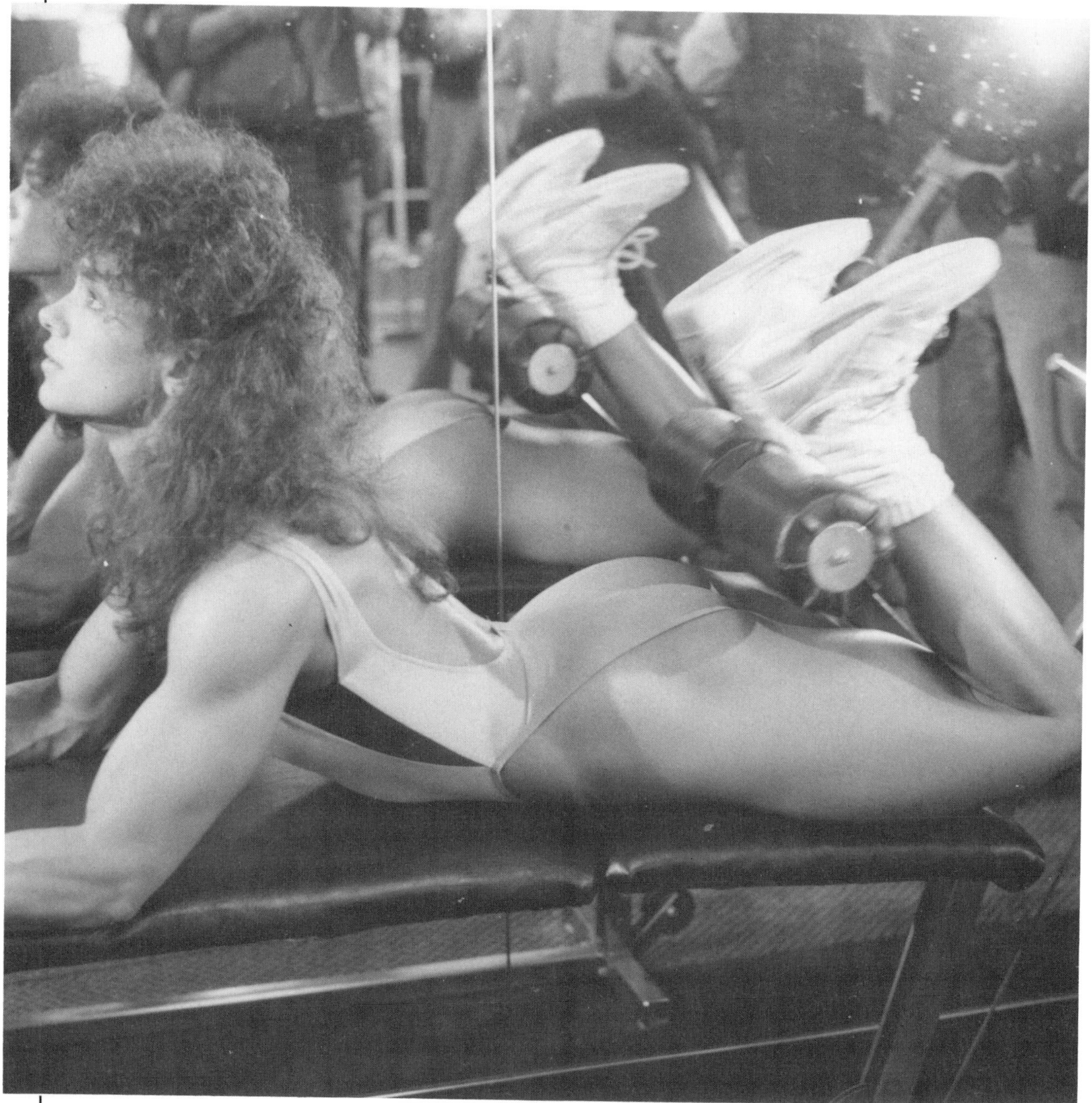

Bronston Austin performs the leg press.

Leg Press

This exercise is performed on a special "leg-press" apparatus. Lie on your back and after placing your feet in position, press the weight upwards. Lower slowly and repeat. The leg press was designed to take the place of the squat which many bodybuilders find uncomfortable. Unfortunately, the leg press, good as it is, does not give the phenomenal results that you get from squats. Some leg-press machines are set at an angle while others are arranged so that you press directly upwards. The 45° leg-press unit is the most popular variation.

No bodybuilder would neglect the lunge in his workout.

Lunges

Stand with feet together with a light barbell across the back of your shoulders held in position by your hands.

Step one pace forward with the left leg and bend it until the left thigh is parallel to the floor, the knee of the right leg almost touching the ground. Keep your upper body and head as erect as possible and return to the feet-together upright position. Next, place the right foot forward and follow the same procedure.

This exercise works the entire thigh area and is particularly useful in stimulating the upper thigh muscles known as thigh "rods."

Thigh Extensions

A special piece of equipment is needed for this movement. Slowly raise and lower the legs, concentrating on the movement at hand. Do not kick the weight up because this allows your muscles to take advantage of the momentum. If they are not made to work hard, they will not build up to the utmost degree. You may exercise both legs together or one at a time. As the legs straighten, hold the contraction for a full second before lowering the resistance.

Rich Gaspari starts thigh extensions (above) and finishes (right).

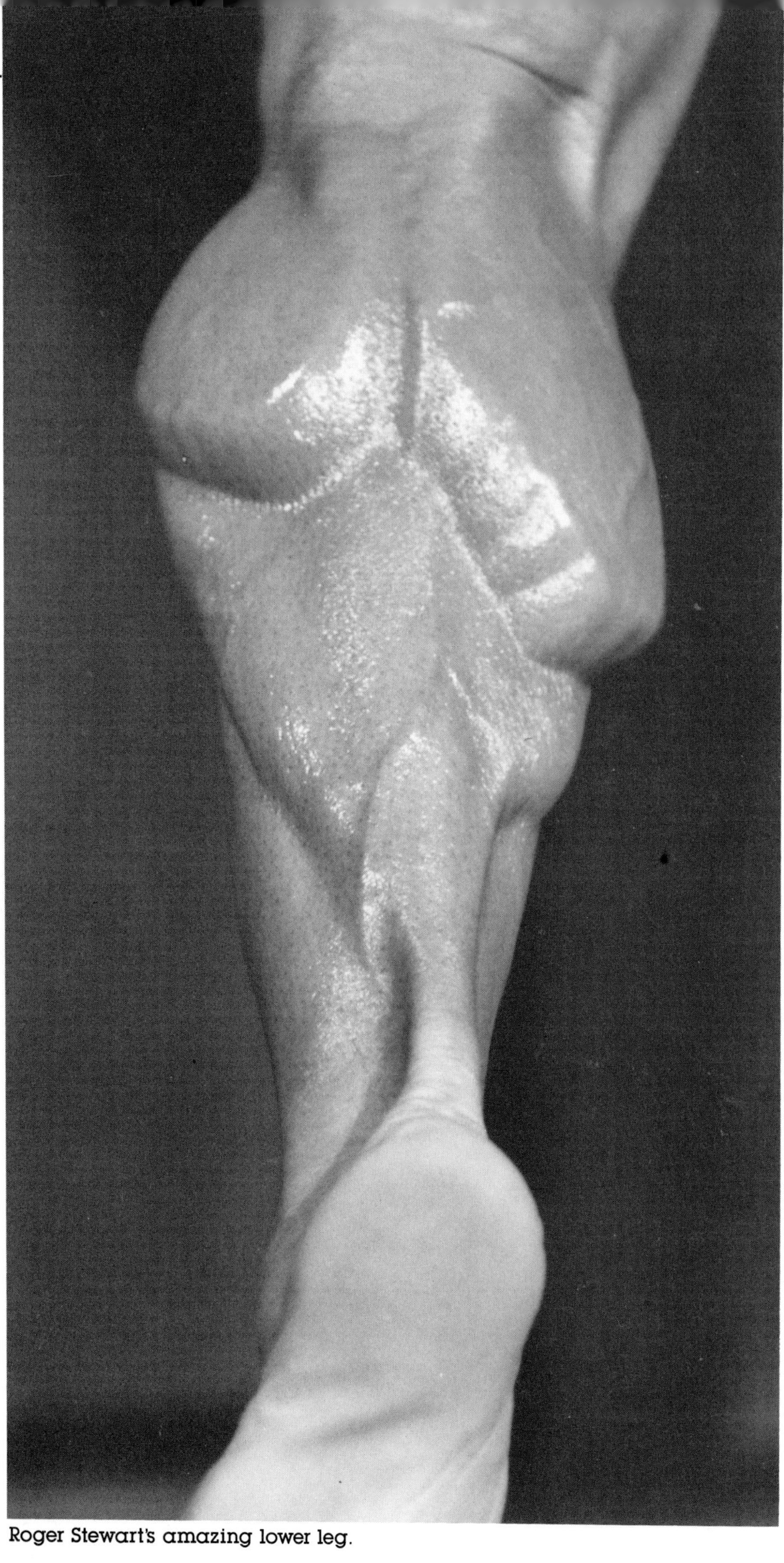

Roger Stewart's amazing lower leg.

CHAPTER 9
CALVES

It used to be a case of "you've either got'em or you haven't." Today, we have more ways to build the lower legs than ever before in the history of bodybuilding. Genetics do, indeed, play an important part in how big and shapely your calves can become. But they are not the whole story. A steady progressively planned program of calf training goes a long way. Calf development doesn't come quickly but it will come. Far better to train your lower legs with 8 to 12 sets two or three times a week than to blitz them every day for a month! Blitzing gives a quick response, but if continued for longer than a week or two the muscle invariably becomes smaller. I remember seeing one bodybuilder (who always competed with very good calf development) on stage, and his calves were almost non-existent. I found out later that this man had blitzed his calves every day for two months with, wait for it, 25 sets per workout! No wonder his calves were 3 inches smaller than their usual measurement.

History has shown that bodybuilders with unimpressive lower leg development can change things around. Witness Reg Park, Arnold Schwarzenegger, and Lou Ferrigno. All three men transformed their lower legs with standing calf-raise machines. In each case, the resistance was built up until well over 500 pounds was used for 15 to 20 repetitions. The first of the three men to work in this way was Park, whose lower legs were definitely underpar. For a short time, Reg actually trained his calves twice a day for 5 days a week. On hearing this, Arnold, too, tried the same system. For a short time it worked but then the Austrian returned to more moderate training and still his lower legs grew.

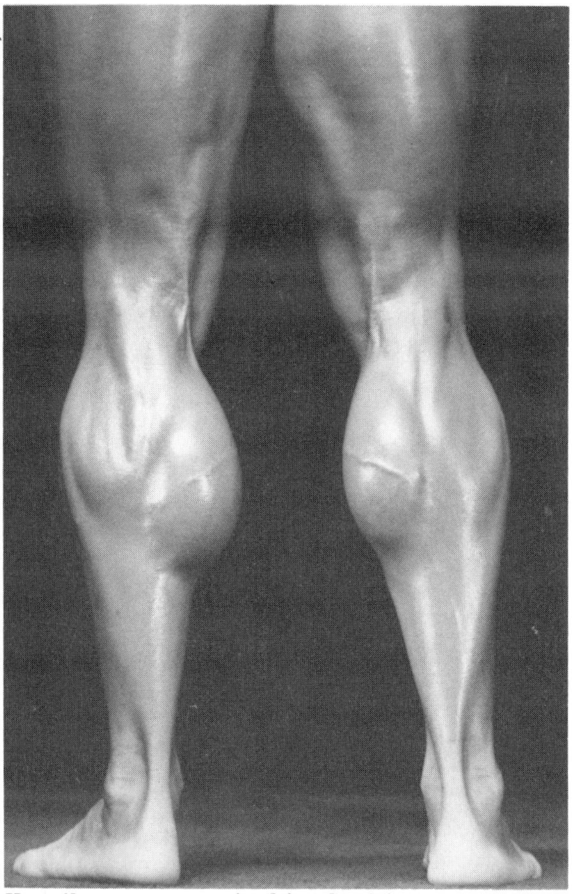

Here they are—surgical implants!

In fact they enlarged so quickly that "Tricky" Ricky Wayne, a regular muscle journalist of the day, started the rumor that the Austrian Oak had given in to the temptation of having calf "implants" inserted.

No, Arnold had not gone the implant route but the technology had arrived and a host of bodybuilders did in fact have surgical implants placed in the lower legs. Among these were Tony Pearson, Alfred Neugebauer (who subsequently had them removed so that he could compete legitimately), the Barbarians, and a dozen amateurs who hope one day to win the Mr. Olympia without their implants being detected. There were even rumors that Mike Christian had calf implants. In fact, while on tour in Europe some of the other professionals insisted that Mike go to the main hospital in Paris to have his legs scanned so that his implants could be identified and Christian could then be banned from competition. Needless to say, Mike was upset at having to undergo these tests, but he did, and the scanning proved without a doubt that Christian had *not* gotten implants.

While bodybuilders with unimpressive lower legs can make improvements, there is the "high-calf" condition that cannot be changed radically. Many black people have this high-knot condition. No amount of exercise will "pull-down" a high calf, although stretching the calf (raising up and down as high and as low as possible, will help slightly). By contrast, Asian people invariably have really good calf development. And if they don't actually have calf mass, they have the *potential* to build it. And talking of "naturals" when I visit Hawaii I'm always amazed at the calf development of most of their bodybuilders. Outstanding!

Not all black people have high calf development. Some of the best calves on earth belong to blacks. The world's most shapely calves belonged to Chris Dickerson. And Bertil Fox, Manny Perry, Vince Taylor, Shawn Ray and a host of other black bodybuilders have exceptional lower leg development. I'll never forget Johnny Fuller's answer to a muscle photographer who was questioning him about his calves. The conversation went like this:

Photographer: Wow! Johnny. Your calves are really great. How long have you been training? And what do they measure?

Fuller: I've been working out for twelve years. My calves measure 19 inches.

Photographer: Wow. 19 inches! That's humungous. What did they measure before you started training as a kid all those years ago?

Fuller: 18 inches!

So you see some blacks do indeed have genetically advantaged lower legs. Johnny Fuller is most definitely one of them.

You should see the things some bodybuilders do to build their calves. I know of at least two guys who slip into their mother's (or wives) high-heel shoes and walk around the yard in the hope that the change of angle will give them added development. Others take up rope jumping, ballet, sprinting in sand—all of these methods may help slightly but the best way is still to employ a system of stretching, followed by the performance of 8 to 10 sets of progressive resistance training on a standing calf machine.

Boyer Coe was one of the earliest advocates of starting a calf-training session with plenty of stretches. "I believe that stretching the calf to increase its range of motion is the most important part of building mass." Boyer will stretch his calves on the 45° leg press and the vertical leg-press machines for up to half an hour before adding significant resistance to the apparatus. Only after he has fully stressed the tendons and ligaments and "maxed the mobility" will he take on the real resistance and pumpout sets of heavy-duty 15 to 20 range repetitions.

Trainer Vince Gironda is very specific about conditions regarding calf training. Hear him: "Always allow for maximum stretch by working from a block that stands at least 6 inches off the floor. This block should be covered with ½-inch layer of glued-on gum rubber padding."

Gironda also believes that it is best to do all calf work barefooted. Trouble with this idea is that when you get into the really big weights, the blocks (padded or not) cut into the feet, making an "all-out" set virtually impossible. The lesson is simple. Use proper exercise shoes when training heavy. You *need* the support they give in order to really work the lower legs fully.

There is a strong trend today for bodybuilders to perform half their calf training sets with the knees bent. This is the method used by Sandy Ridell. And nobody works their lower legs more completely than this woman. Bending the knees may seem more awkward but it gives a "different" effect, and the blood circulation is enhanced when the knees are unlocked.

I remember one young bodybuilder (with 15-inch calves) telling Arnold Schwarzenegger how he trained his calves using light weights and very high reps. "I get a real burn," he told Arnold. "Listen," replied the Austrian. "If I lit a match under your behind you'd get a real burn, but that doesn't mean you'd get bigger!" We all laughed, but Arnold had made his point. Stretch and then work heavy and hard for maximum calf development.

Donkey Calf Raise

There is no doubt that the "bent-over" position one adopts for the donkey calf raise exercise does something very special for the lower legs. This is a great favorite of Mr. Olympia Frank Zane.

Lean on a bench or table top so that your upper body is comfortably supported parallel to the floor. A training partner sits on your lower back, over the hip area. Rise up and down on your toes, until you cannot perform another rep. Use a 4-inch block under the toes to give greater range to the foot movement. You should always aim to perform at least 20 reps in this exercise.

Standing Calf Raise

It is important that the calf machine you use is capable of loading on heavy weights. The apparatus should either carry a huge stack of weights or else be set up with a leverage benefit so that comparatively small amounts of weight give considerably increased overall load.

Rise up and down on your toes without excessive knee bend and without bouncing at the bottom of the movement.

Seated Calf Raise

This exercise, too, is performed on a special leverage machine. The principal muscle worked in this movement is the *soleus* rather than the *gastrocnemius*. Perform as many heel raises as you can, concentrating on maximizing total calf stretch with each repetition.

Leg Press Machine Calf Raise

Calf raises may also be performed on the leg press machine. Some of these machines are set at an angle while others are set up so that the movement is performed lying on the back with legs vertical. Get as much extension as possible with this exercise, pointing the toes as much as possible in the "up" position and lowering them as far as possible in the "down" position.

Jon-Jon Park gives Larry Scott some resistance to work with in the donkey calf raise.

Steve Davis at the start and finish of the calf raise.

Tom Platz on the seated calf machine.

Ali Mala doing the leg press.

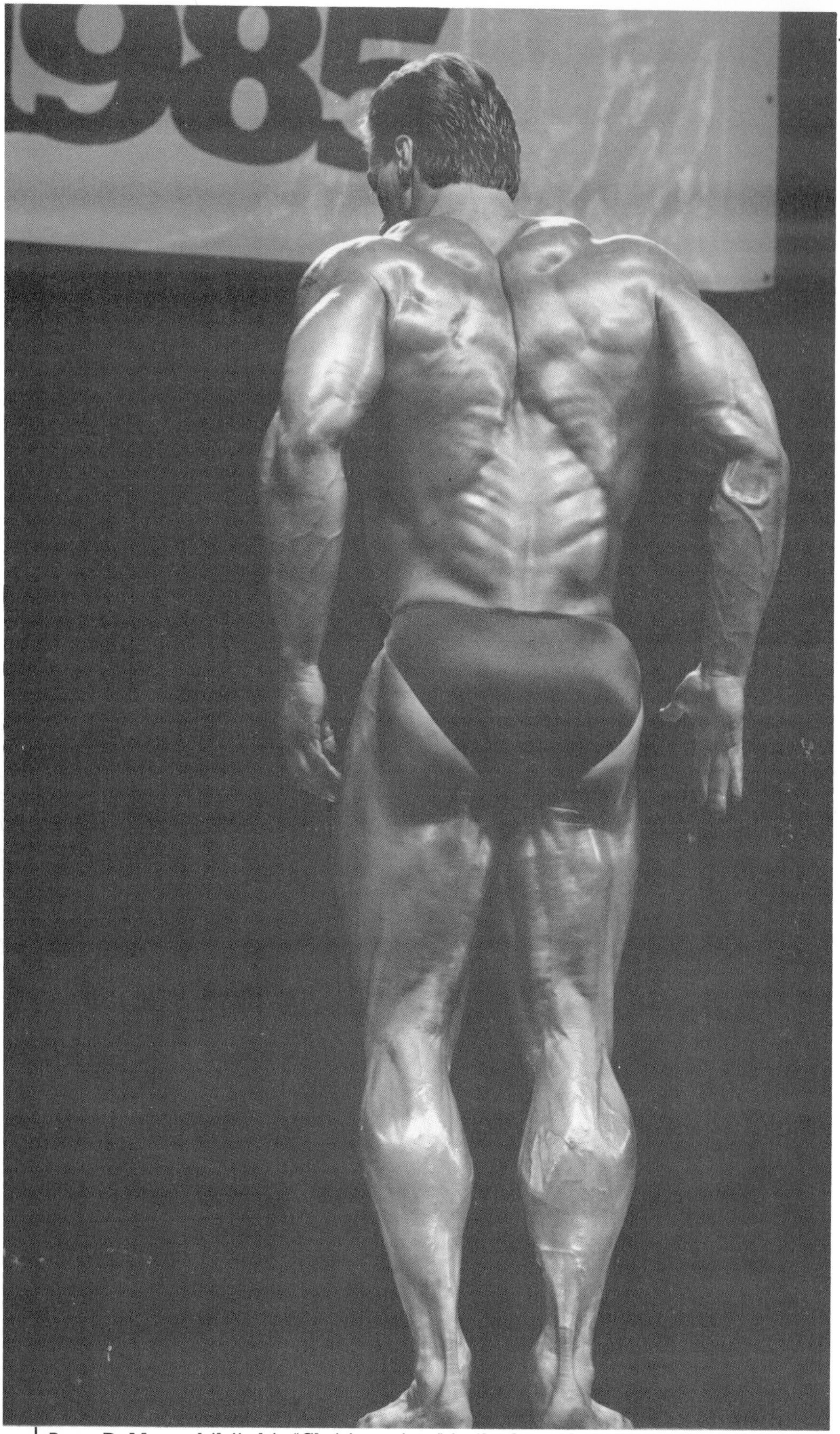

Berry DeMey exhibits his "Christmas tree" in the lower back.

CHAPTER 10
LOWER BACK AND GLUTES

The lower back is not one of the most visual parts of the body. Certainly when a friend asks to see our muscles we don't turn around and show our lower back muscles. It's far more likely that we flex a biceps or tighten our abs. But the lower back is an important muscle area. It is judged in bodybuilding competitions and its development is important for health and vitality.

When beginners first learn to lift a weight from the floor they are taught to keep the back flat, bend the knees, and lift with the hips. This lesson, once learned, must never be forgotten because if you lift a barbell or pair of dumbbells in any other way you run the risk of lower back injury. In fact, incorrect lifting of *any* object can lead to lower back muscle tears or even worse, a cartilage or disc problem.

When lifting a weight always make sure it is kept as close to the body as possible. Attempt to lift with the thighs and hips rather than the arms. Many a lumbar region has been "strained" by trying to lift an object that is not sufficiently close to your center of gravity.

Today, we have the lower-back phenomenon known as "the Christmas tree." This was first dramatically brought to our attention by Samir Bannout when he won the 1983 Mr. Olympia in Munich, Germany. Other bodybuilders have since learned to bring out their Christmas tree striations to shock the international judging panels. The best lower-back Christmas-tree effect probably belongs to Holland's Berry DeMey.

The amazingly defined lower lats of Lance Dreher.

Yup! The glutes are muscles too! In the first edition of *Hardcore Bodybuilding* I left this area alone. In those far-off days (1982), it was considered that this sensitive area took care of itself if we trained hard on all-round leg and lower back exercises. Pose trunks were not all that brief in those days and the behind was pretty well covered.

Rachel McLish was the first person to partially uncover her glute muscles in competition. The act definitely gave her an edge with the judges. She had always trained her butt vigorously and had built quite outstanding muscle and contour in the region. Rachel quickly became a double Ms. Olympia winner. Other women competitors followed suit. They specifically trained their glute muscles and subsequently showed them off onstage like any other muscle group. While all this was going on, the men kept their glute muscles well hidden until a young Richard Gaspari one night turned his back on the audience at Wayne DeMilia's *Night of Champions*, raised his pose suit up, and flexed what were to go down in bodybuilding history as the first ripped glutes. Today many men and quite a few women display this same amazing condition at contests.

Building and shaping the behind is now part of bodybuilding. True enough leg exercises such as squats, deadlifts and leg curls have a spill-over effect, but bodybuilding is now more specialized than ever, and we have a variety of movements to build and shape the glute muscles.

Rear Low Cable Kickback (Glutes)

Stand facing a cable machine. Attach the strap to the ankle and fix it to the low cable pulley. Holding onto an upright for support, raise your leg backwards. Keep it straight throughout the movement. Return and repeat. Work each leg for 12 to 15 repetitions before putting the cable strap on the other leg and repeating the performance.

Rachel McLish performs the rear low cable kickback.

"Good Morning" Exercise (Lower Back)

Place a light barbell across the back of your shoulders, and with your legs comfortably apart, lean forward at the waist. Keep the knees locked, back flat and head up. It is important that you hold tightly onto the barbell. Dip as low as possible without undue discomfort, straighten up and repeat.

Tim Belknap, 1981's Mr. America, begins the "good morning" exercise (left) and completes the movement (below).

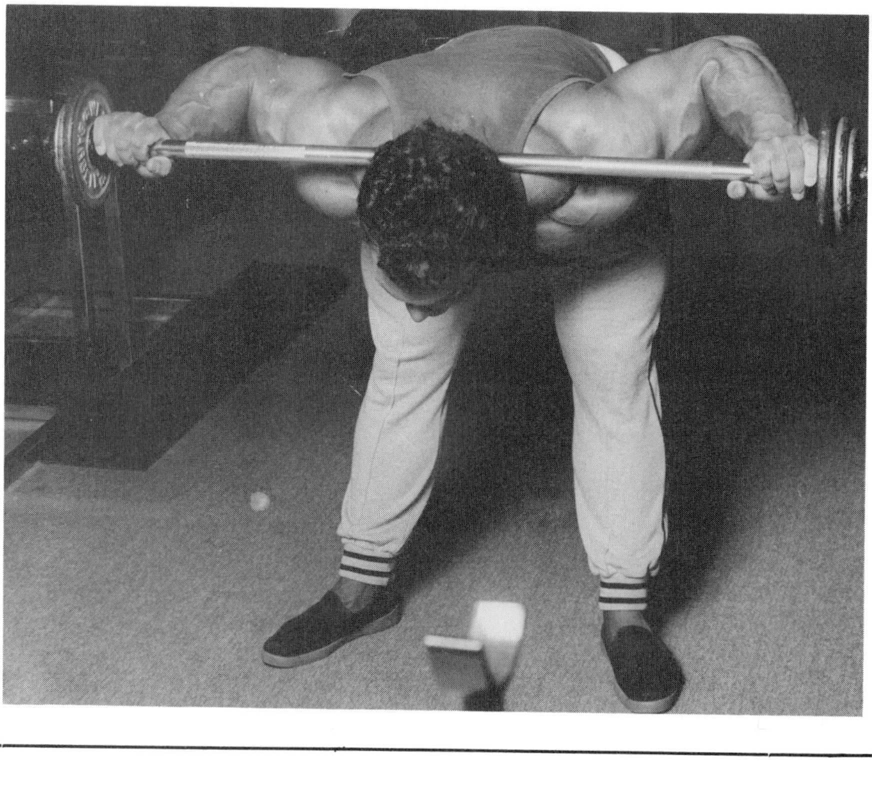

Casey Viator works on the stiff leg deadlift while standing on one end of the exercise bench.

Stiff Leg Deadlift (Lower Back and Upper Glutes)

Stand erect at one end of an exercise bench, holding a light barbell in the arms-down position. Bend forward so that the weight is lowered to the toes, raise, and repeat. Keep your head up at all times. This exercise works the hamstrings as well as the lumbar region and the upper areas of the butt. Never attempt to use heavy weights in this exercise.

Tom Platz begins the deadlift (top) and finishes (bottom).

The Deadlift (Lower Back and Glutes)

Stand over the barbell with the bar touching against the front of the lower legs. Grab the bar with an alternate grip (one hand undergrip, one hand overgrip), hands about 2 feet apart. Bend over the bar, back flat, bottom out, knees bent, head up. Now, without bending your arms, lift the weight from the floor, until your body is completely upright. Lower and repeat, bearing in mind as you do that you must never cease to adopt this important flat-back position.

Prone Hyperextension (Lower Back and Glutes)

This is performed on an exercise unit especially designed for the job. Until recently, it was performed from a high bench or table. Place the legs and hips, front downwards, on the exercise unit. The upper body should be free to rise up and down. Place your hands behind your head and lower your trunk towards the floor. Rise until your body is in a straight line. Lower, and repeat. In time, as your lumbar region strengthens, you may hold a barbell behind your head as in the "Good Morning" exercise. This movement is probably the best lower back exercise of all.

The main spill-over exercises that have a positive effect on the glutes include upper leg movement like squats, leg presses, and leg curls, and lower back moves like prone hyperextensions and Good Mornings. Obviously additional glute involvement in these exercises can be directed into the area by slight position adjustments and even by concentrating on making the glute muscles take on the stress of the exercise rather than the legs or lower back.

Likewise, when you want to concentrate on the lumbar region you should put your mind into *feeling* the stress in that area exclusively. As you can see from the exercises listed in this chapter, there is a strong correlation between the lower back and the butt. Many movements work both areas equally.

Steve Brisbois demonstrates the prone hyperextension exercise on the special unit designed for it.

Gary Strydom's superior deltoid development.

CHAPTER 11
SHOULDERS

Broad shoulders have a magic of their own. Every romance novel hero, every cowboy, every private eye, every Indian chief, every leading man has them. And what about you?

Your natural clavicle width (the bi-acromial measurement) is dependent on how selective you were in choosing your parents, but even if you have inherited narrow shoulders, you can do something about the problem. Deltoid muscle mass can be built and it can be built quickly. Enlarging the muscle can add greatly to shoulder impressiveness. This is particularly true if you build the side head of the shoulders. There are in fact three heads to the shoulders—the rear head (posterior deltoid) the front head (anterior deltoid) and the side head (lateral deltoid). All three areas should be worked vigorously, but because of its widening effect you should put most of your effort into building the side deltoid area.

Can you widen the bi-acromial width? Only slightly. This comes about from all-round bodybuilding, especially the overhead pressing of weights. Many hand balancers, because of the support-stress placed on the shoulders, have wider clavicles than average. The straight-arm pullover puts a special kind of pressure on the clavicle which tends to widen them if the movement is practiced faithfully for a period of months. To perform the straight-arm pullover, lie on a bench, face up. Hold a light bar, 20 to 25 pounds, at arm's length perpendicular to your torso. Keep your feet flat on the ground on either side of the bench. Your hands should be shoulder-width apart. Breathe in deeply through the mouth and lower the bar (keeping your arms straight) behind your head until it almost touches to floor. Raise the bar to the start position, breathing out as you do so. Repeat 12 to 20 repetitions.

In days of old, bodybuilders would only work their deltoids with basic overhead pressing movements. Very few people, indeed, would work the individual heads for a completely balanced appearance. Today, especially if you plan to one day enter contests, you *have* to develop all three deltoid sections. Here are the reasons why you need to develop all three deltoid areas.

SIDE (LATERAL DELTOID)

This is the part of your shoulders that actually adds width. Just an inch on either side and you will completely change your appearance. If you doubt me try this simple test. Slip into a tight sweat or tee shirt and place a rolled-up sock or handkerchief underneath the sweater on the outer sides of each shoulder. Now take a look at the mirror. Just an inch more width either side and you look like Hercules unchained!

REAR (POSTERIOR) DELTOID

Development of the back of your shoulders is a must. It greatly improves your postural appearance, preventing you from looking round-shouldered. It also gives you shoulder thickness from the side, and when viewed relaxed from the rear, well-developed posterior deltoids add that important detail to overall back impressiveness.

FRONT (ANTERIOR) DELTOID

It used to be fashionable to "tie in" the front deltoids with the upper pecs. This was accomplished with plenty of incline barbell presses and facilitated by the fact that bodybuilding had higher percentages of fat in former days.

Today, pec tie-ins are out. Rather than trying to develop pecs that flow into the delts, today's bodybuilders build the pecs as one muscle, and work the front deltoid as a separate area. This separation actually aids the upper body appearance and, contrary to popular opinion, a bulging front deltoid helps your "visual" width because any form of cross lighting will show it up as a separate entity and the ultimate visual effect is broader shoulders.

Most people enjoy working the shoulders. There are a variety of pushing and pulling motions that exercise the delts, and the shoulders respond well in most cases. They get a good pump, and growth is normally fairly rapid.

All forms of pressing movements, while in the upright position, strenuously work the shoulders. Olympic lifters involved in pressing and jerking heavy weights overhead invariably have large, well rounded shoulders.

It is often a good idea to start off your shoulder routine with several sets of heavy (quality) shoulder work, such as the press-behind-neck exercise, and conclude the routine with isolation exercises such as lateral raises, front raises, etc., but it is the variety and "shockability" of your routines that keep the muscles growing. A complete reversal of procedure often stimulates additional growth.

Lateral Raise

Seated or standing, the lateral raise can be performed effectively in numerous ways. You may experiment to find out which way is most effective for you.

One proven method is to start with two dumbbells held in front of the thighs (side by side, touching). Raise the dumbbells out to the side, keeping the arms slightly bent as you do so. As the dumbbells rise upwards, turn the wrists downwards, as though you were pouring water out of the end of the weight (little fingers uppermost). Lower, and repeat. You may work one arm at a time if you wish, as Tom Platz does or as Roy Callender does with a cable.

Ron Love starts the lateral raise (left) and completes the movement (below).

Rich Gaspari performs the two-hand dumbbell press, starting at the left and finishing below.

Two-Hand Dumbbell Press

This may be performed either seated or standing. Start with the dumbbells held at shoulder level, palms facing inward. Press the weights simultaneously overhead, lower and repeat.

A variation of this exercise is the "Arnold" press which I first saw performed by Larry Scott, two years before Arnold had started weight training. This variation is commenced with the dumbbells held at the shoulder, but knuckles facing forward (as though you had just curled the weights.)

As you begin to press upwards, the movement in this particular variation involves twisting the wrists so that the knuckles twist from facing frontwards to the full twist position when they end up back-to-back at the conclusion of the press, as the dumbbells are at arm's length above the head. Lower and repeat.

The alternate dumbbell press (start at left, finish below) as executed by Tim Belknap.

Alternate Dumbbell Press

This exercise, too, can be performed in either the standing or sitting position. Simply raise first one dumbbell, then the other in an alternating style.

This exercise differs from the two-handed version in that the body is not inclined to lean back during the performance, which is definitely the case in the regular dumbbell press.

Brad Verret begins (left) the alternate dumbbell forward raise and finishes (below).

Alternate Dumbbell Forward Raise

Holding two dumbbells alternately raise one, then the other, straight forward, until each is taken past the horizontal position. This exercise works the anterior (frontal) area of the shoulders.

Bent-Over Flying

This may be performed seated on the end of a bench, or merely in the bent-over position. Try to keep the body more or less parallel to the floor. Raise the dumbbells upwards as high as possible and lower slowly. The arms should be bent slightly at the elbow throughout the movement. Raise and lower slowly.

The start of the bent-over flying exercise (right) and the finish (below) as performed by John Terilli.

In the upright row exercise, Tom Platz holds the row bar forward.

Upright Row

To properly work the shoulder muscles and not the trapezius, you should grasp the barbell with hands shoulder-width apart.

Raise and lower the bar, palms facing down, elbows held as high as possible throughout the exercise. Keep the action rhythmic. You may hold the barbell out away from the body during this exercise if you wish. It puts a little more "constant" tension on the deltoid muscles.

Rear Delt Machine

The posterior deltoids may also be worked using the rear delt machine. Clench the hands strongly and pull back firmly as far as possible. Return and repeat.

Steve Brisbois works on the rear delt machine.

Brad Verret in three stages of the press-behind-neck (above and opposite).

Press-Behind-Neck (from Racks)

Although it is not absolutely necessary, you will find that you get better results by placing the loaded barbell on squat racks prior to doing the press-behind-neck. This eliminates the energy-consuming cleaning of the weight (bringing it from floor to shoulders), plus the wasted motion of getting it into position behind your neck.

Duck under the bar, with your hands set about 28 to 32 inches apart. Press upwards while standing or sitting erect, being careful to hold your elbows back throughout the movement. As soon as the arms straighten, return and repeat. Some people prefer to lock out (lock the elbows as arms straighten) each rep while others feel this is unnecessary. Both styles work and whether or not you choose to lock out is up to you. After the set, return the barbell to the racks.

SHOULDER BUILDING ROUTINES

Routine One

Exercise	Sets	Reps
Press-Behind-Neck	4	8
Lateral Raise	4	12–15
Bentover Flying	4	12
Alternate Forward Dumbbell Raise	4	12–15

Routine Two

Upright Rowing } Alternate	4	12
Two-Hand Dumbbell Press 1 } Alternate		
Rear delt machine	4	15

Routine Three

Alternate Dumbbell Press	4	8–10
Lateral Raise with Cable	3	15
Bentover Flying	3	15

Routine Four

Alternate Forward Raise	4	12
Seated Lateral Raise	4	12
Bentover Flying	4	12

Routine Five

Lateral Raise } Alternate	4	12
Press-Behind-Neck 1 } Alternate		
Rear Delt Machine	3	10–15
Upright Rowing	3	10–15

44 LBS
WEIDER
WORLD

44 LBS
WEIDER
WORLD

Gary Strydom exhibits amazing chest development.

CHAPTER 12
CHEST

Everybody has differently shaped pecs. Look at the pectoral muscles from the front: Some have a straight across lower pec line; others have a rounded curve under each pectoral. And, whichever category you fall into cannot be changed. But the muscle mass in the various sections *can* be changed, at least slightly.

THE UPPER PECTORALS

This area is best built with all forms of incline bench exercises. Set the angle between 35 and 50°. A steep incline will work the top of the chest. The lower the incline, the further down the effect will be.

Experiment with a variety of movements including incline barbell bench presses, incline dumbbell presses and incline flyes with dumbbells or pulleys.

THE INNER PECTORALS

Today, bodybuilders want to show plenty of development around the sternum (the chest bone). Also, when the inner chest is built maximally, the pec striations are more likely to show up dramatically.

The inner pectorals used to be hard to train, but today we have specialized apparatus, which includes the cable crossover exercise (the inner pecs are best attacked by crossing the arms over in the front of the body at the conclusion of each rep) and the Pek-Dek movement, in which the forearms are squeezed together each repetition.

Janice Ragain.

THE OUTER PECTORALS

The outer pec is the most neglected section, and most men and women bodybuilders need development in this area. Why? Because when you build the outer pectorals you greatly enhance the flair of the physique. You create the added illusion of width in the upper chest and shoulder region. Without muscle in the upper, outer area of the chest you will have a pinched-in or bunched-up look to the chest.

The best outer chest exercises are the wide grip dips on the parallel bars (chin on chest, elbows out, feet forward of the body), the wide grip barbell bench press and the flat flye exercise with dumbbells.

It's interesting to note that along with the hips (glutes and upper thighs) the pectorals are among the fastest-growing muscles. For this reason one should always be aware of the problem of stretch marks. If you are susceptible to these "skin tears," then do not combine lots of heavy pectoral exercises with a high-calorie food intake. Stretch marks are not curable. They are the result of muscle outgrowing the capacity of the skin to expand adequately to accommodate the growth. Proper nutrition, especially minerals, may help keep the elasticity of the skin in tiptop condition. The only answer to stretch-mark eradication is surgery, so your best protection against this unsightly condition is to not get them in the first place.

Many people want to know if they can increase the size of their rib cage. This will come about from adding muscular body weight, but you help things along a bit by practicing straight-arm pullovers (using a light barbell) or across the bench dumbbell pullovers. Traditionally, the old physical culture school of bodybuilding recommended that rib cage size was built by alternating sets of high rep (breathing) squats (20–30 reps) with light pullovers. Did it work? For some, with already roomy rib cages it worked, but the thin ectomorphic bodybuilders with narrow rib cages seldom showed much permanent expansion.

Pullovers do help but only slightly. You might get better results from deep breathing and posing (filling the lungs with air and lifting the rib cage).

Bench Press

The king of weight training moves, the noble bench press, is by far the most popular exercise. As you are lying on your back, feet firmly planted on the floor, a training partner can hand you the barbell, or you can take it from the rack at the head of the bench. Lower to the nipple area of the chest, and push to arm's length overhead, keeping your elbows outward as far from the trunk as possible. Lower and repeat. Be sure not to let the weight bounce from the chest as this could damage the delicate nerve center beneath it. This movement may also be done with dumbbells.

Steve Brisbois shows the start (right) and finish (below) of the bench press.

Bronston Austin at the start of the Pek-Dek crunches (above) and the conclusion (right).

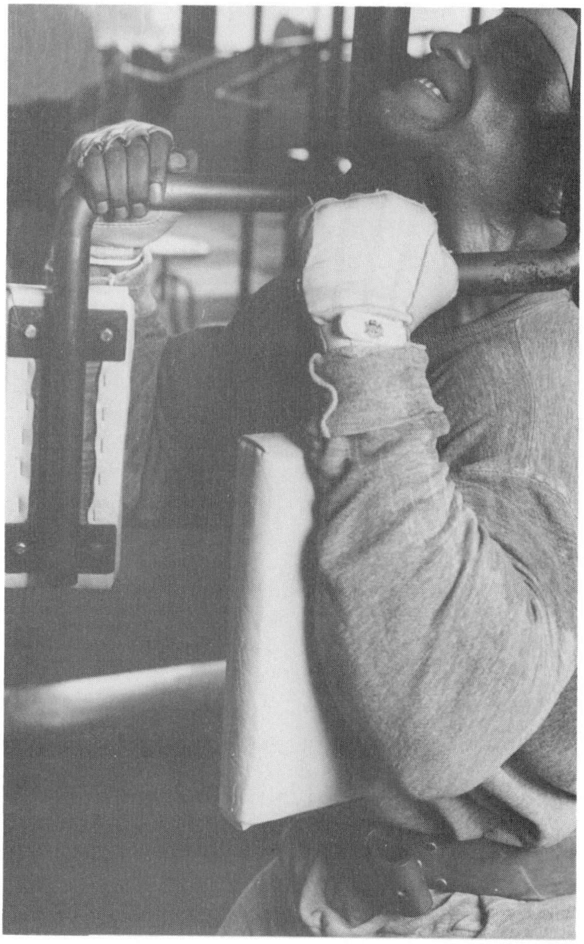

Pek-Dek Crunches

You need a special Pek-Dek machine for this one. Hold the apparatus securely, starting with the elbows out to the side. Concentrate hard and close the elbows together. Return, and repeat. This is an isolation pec exercise and works the entire pectoral area.

Flying

Lie on your back with two dumbbells (or cables) held in the arms-straight position overhead. Lower slowly out to the side of the body (arms at right angles to the torso) as far as possible, raise, and repeat. The elbows should be slightly bent throughout the movement, but should not alter position during the exercise (imagine your arm locked in a cast). Substantial weight can be used in this exercise after some practice. It may also be done on an incline bench.

Tom Platz shows how he works his pectorals with the flying exercise.

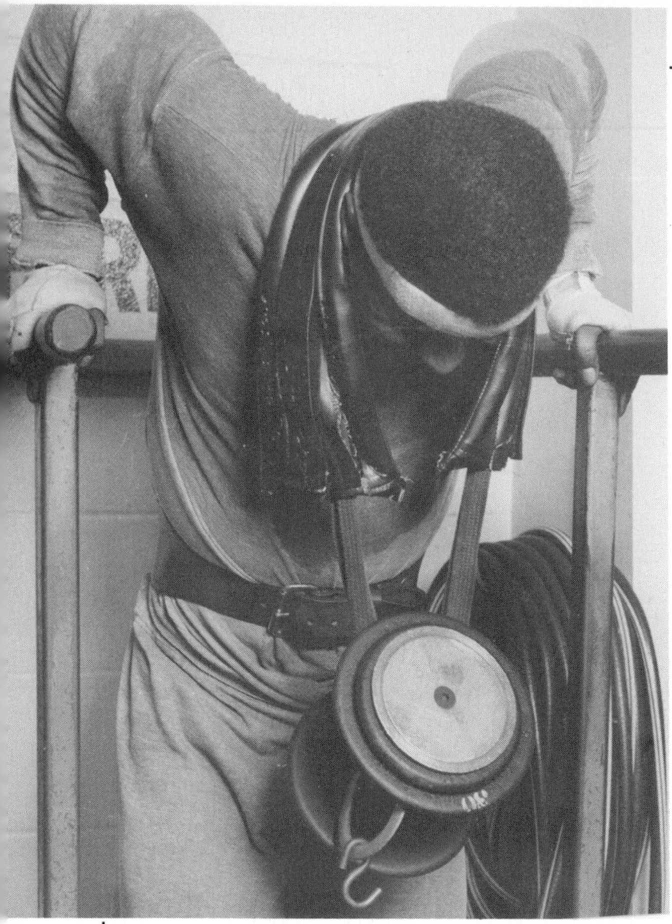

Wide-Grip Dips

Vince Gironda said that the largest pecs he ever saw were on old-time iron man Bill Trumbo. "He never did bench presses," said Vince, "only dips."

Gironda's way of performing parallel bar dips is unique and definitely workable in that it builds the pecs out at the sides (outer line) which gives an overall impression of chest width, enhancing the general "V" shape.

Your hands should be at least 31 inches apart; if you are tall, make it 33 inches apart. Throughout the dipping motion it is important to keep feet forward, chin on chest, and elbows out to the side of the body. (This is a completely different movement from regular triceps dips which, although also done on parallel bars, are performed with elbows close to the body, feet tucked under the torso, and head up.)

Stretch down as far as you can, and raise. You will feel the effect in the pectorals after a few sets.

Bronston Austin starts the wide-grip dip (above) and finishes the movement (below).

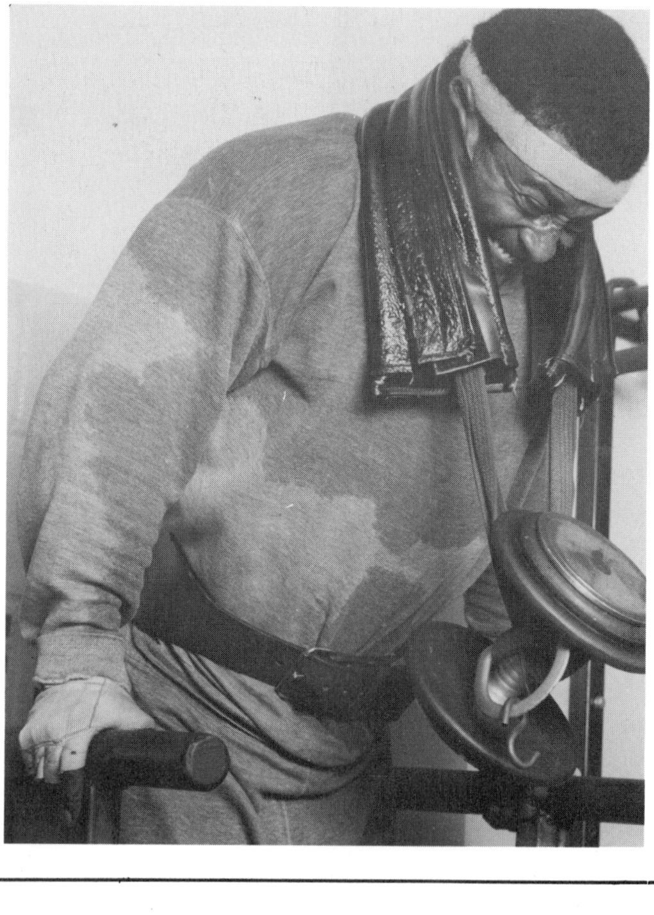

Tonya Knight spots Marjo Selin on the incline bench press.

Incline Bench Press

Hold two dumbbells (or barbells) at arm's length above the head while lying on an incline bench. Usually the bench is placed at a 45° angle, but more of the pectoral is worked if the bench is set at a shallower angle, around 35° being ideal. Keeping the arms out to the sides (elbows back) and palms facing forward, lower the weights to the chest, raise, and repeat. You may also do this with a barbell "Smith" machine.

Dumbbell Pullover

Some may argue that this is more a lat exercise than a chest movement. It does work the lat area, but credit is more often given to the movement for mobilizing the rib cage and working the upper pectorals. Start by lying across an exercise bench, supporting the upper back only. Hold a single dumbbell in both hands above your head so that it is supported comfortably (and safely) in the vertical position. Lower slowly behind the head, keeping your arms slightly bent. Allow the rib cage to stretch fully, and return again to the arms-straight position above the head. A light barbell can be substituted for the dumbbell if preferred. Use a shoulder-width grip.

The start of the dumbbell pullover (left) and the conclusion (below) as performed by Roy Callender.

Mike Christian starts the pulley crossover (above) and ends (below).

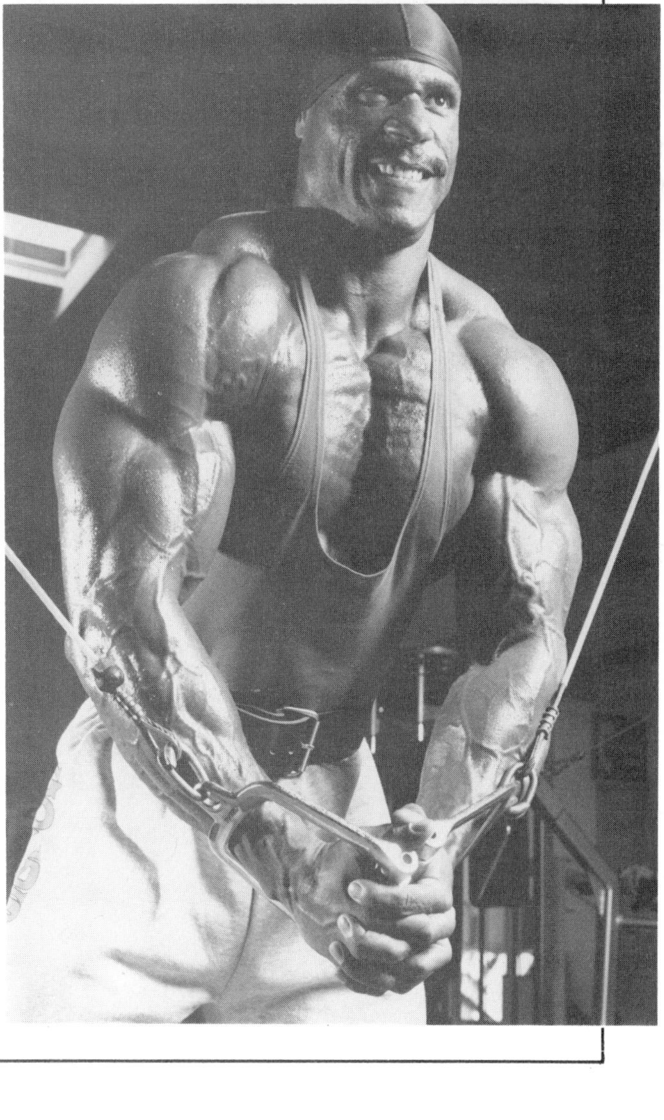

Pulley Crossover

Most gyms have pulley crossover apparatus, although the item would be considered a luxury in a home gym setup. Properly applied, cable crossovers can enable you to work the center area of the chest in a way difficult to reach with any other form of exercise apparatus, except perhaps the Pek-Dek.

Hold the pulley handles in an initial "crucifix" position, and, leaning slightly forward, bring your hands together in front of the body. Your elbows should be fixed in a slightly bent position (that plaster cast again). Experiment with your body and hand positions to direct the maximum amount of effort into the chest region.

What a back! It belongs to Mike Christian.

CHAPTER 13 BACK

When an advanced bodybuilder really wants to show a large amount of awesome muscle there is seldom any better way than to twist the torso and perform a double biceps pose from the rear. "The back displays beautifully," says Arnold Schwarzenegger. And he should know. He won 7 Mr. Olympia titles and was generally considered to have one of the most awesome back developments of all time. For most of his career, Arnold had little difficulty in defending his Mr. Olympia crown. But if he felt the competition breathing down the back of his neck, the Austrian would quickly swoop into his famous "three-quarter back" pose and kill off any real or imagined threat.

Best backs in bodybuilding today include Mike Christian, Tony Pearson, Aaron Baker, Mike Quinn, Lance Dreher, and Lee Haney.

There are two aspects to back development. You have to devote specific attention (exercises) to building back width (the 'V' shape). Additionally you should adopt special movements to build back thickness.

BACK WIDTH

This is principally a matter of pulling out the scapula, the shoulder blades. These bones are mobilized in exercises involving lat machines and chin bars.

After years in bodybuilding, judging contests, writing books, and publishing *MuscleMag International*, I am utterly convinced that the best back-widening exercise of all is the wide-grip-chin-behind-neck. On the surface, this movement may appear to be exactly the same as the wide-grip pulldown. Not so. For starters, the upper arms are pulled towards the lower arms in the chin. In the pulldown the opposite is the case. Secondly, when we chin, we have to hold onto the bar with a minimum weight force of our entire body weight. The lat machine advocate can relieve pressure by "resting" his resistance. Thirdly, the chin is a direct "straight down" gravity pull. In the pulldown

Gary Leonard helps Krista Anderson in the wide-grip chin behind the neck.

the body angle is often changed to relieve stress, making the exercise less intense. There are bodybuilders who don't chin, who only use lat machines and rows. And their backs show it! On the other hand, you can always tell a back that has been subjected to lots of chins. It looks more rugged, more built, and definitely has superior shape.

I don't mean to knock the lat pulldown machine. It has its uses, especially in the wide variety of angles that can be used. It can be especially useful if you go over to the lat machine *immediately* after getting your final rep on the chin bar. Perform another 10 reps with a lighter resistance. Gives a great pump!

BACK THICKNESS

This is best achieved with bent-over rowing movements. But you have to be careful with this exercise because when you bend over and hold a heavy weight at the same time, you could be inviting lower back injury. For this reason, never use monumental weights and always "pull" the weight into your stomach, not to the chest as some people advocate. Actually, lifting to the waist involves the belly of the lat muscle more than does lifting to the chest.

You can perform free weight rows with a barbell, but a superior movement is the T-bar row where the weight is fixed at one end. It will be less likely to injure your lower back too. The single arm dumbbell row is also a good back thickener, as is the seated pulley row movement.

Lats come in all shapes and sizes. Two conditions prevail most commonly. Those who have "high" lats and those who have so called "low" lats. Both need to be corrected as much as possible. Those who have low lats should stress exercises like wide-grip chins and wide-grip pulldowns. If you have high lats, then always "pull" the resistance into the hip area rather than the chest when performing rows or seated pulley exercises. As in so many cases, you cannot transform the natural inclination of your lats to be "high" or "low" but you can make a slight difference; and usually that's enough to give your back a championship appearance.

Wide-Grip Chin

Grasp an overhead bar using an overgrip (palms down) at least a foot wider than your shoulders on either side. (If your shoulders are 2 feet across, take a grip about 4 feet wide.)

Pull upwards, keeping your elbows back throughout the movement. You may pull up so that the bar is in front or behind your neck. This is entirely up to you. Some bodybuilders like to change around for variety, but it would not be correct to say that one form is superior to the other.

Lower until your arms are straight, and repeat. Once you can perform 12 to 15 reps, it is a good idea to attach added weight with the help of a weight belt after which you can build up your reps again.

Arnold Schwarzenegger shows the start of the bent-over rowing exercise.

Bent-Over Rowing

This is one of the most popular exercises for putting some meat on your lats. Grab a barbell with hands about 24 inches apart. Bend your knees slightly and keep your head as high as possible while bending your torso parallel to the floor. Keep your lower back flat, your seat stuck outward, and pull up vigorously on the bar. Pull it into the tummy, not the chest. Lower until arms are completely stretched, and more. Do not rest the weight on the floor until the set is completed. Pull up and repeat. Some bodybuilders prefer to use a single dumbbell, working one arm at a time. The effect is slightly different, and may, in fact, safeguard you from back injury. This is a real possibility with regular barbell rowing, especially if you are predisposed to back trouble or are using weights that are just too heavy. This exercise may also be done using one end of a bar as shown by Sergio Oliva. (This exercise is also known as T-bar rowing.)

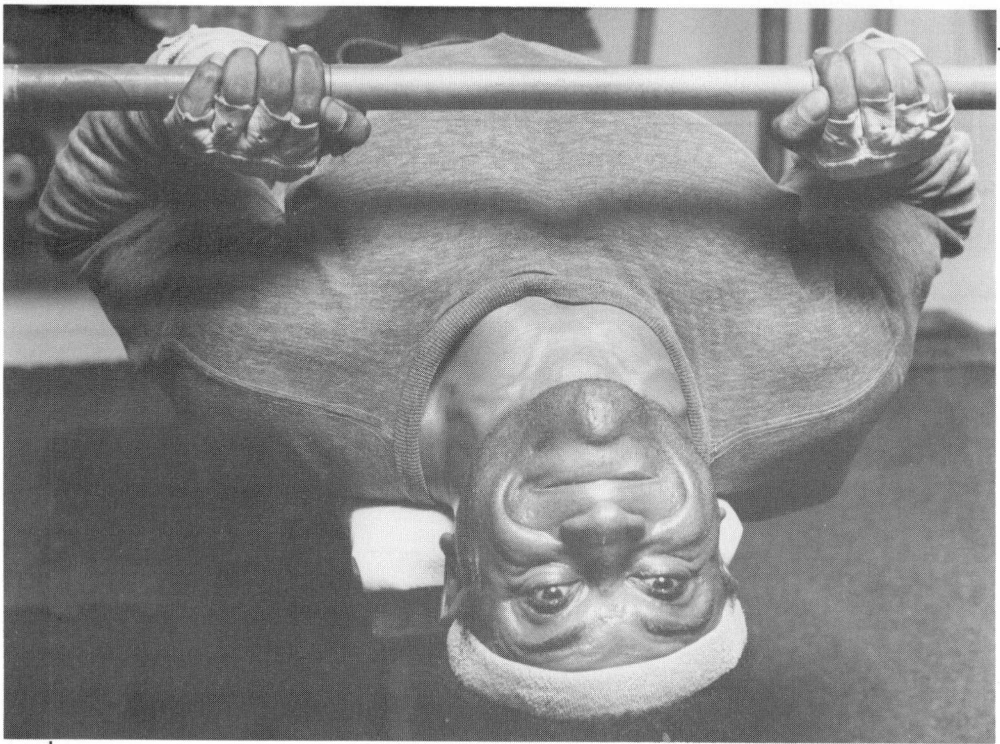

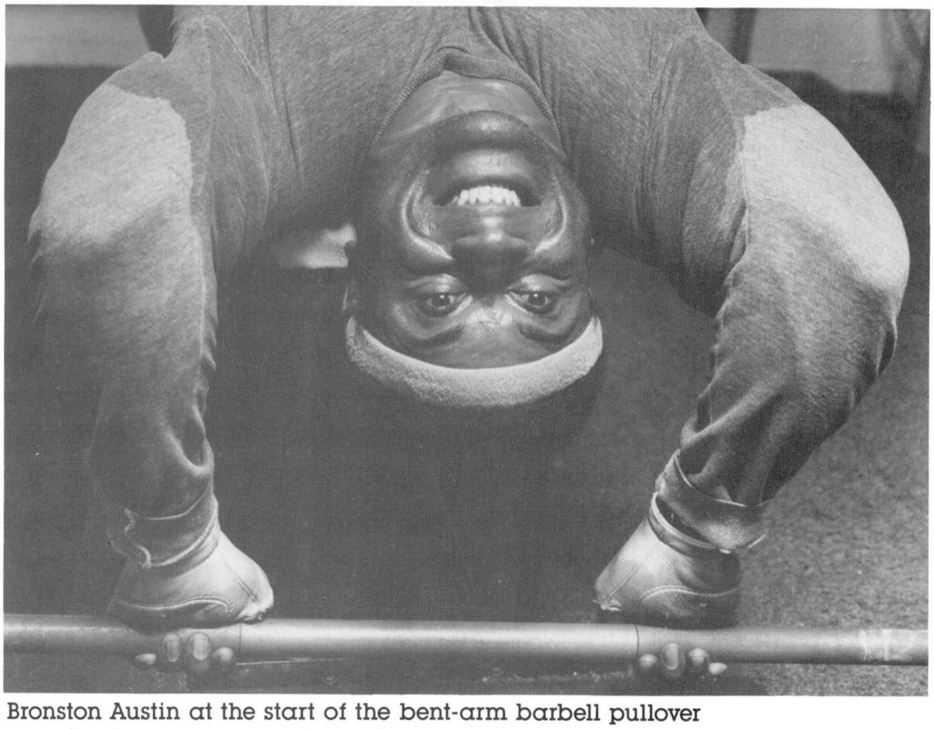

Bronston Austin at the start of the bent-arm barbell pullover exercise (top) and at the finish (bottom).

Bent-Arm Barbell Pullover

Lie flat on an exercise bench with your head hanging over the end. Hold a barbell with a grip of between 12 and 14 inches. Start with the bar held at the chest and lower it slowly behind the head. Concentrate on feeling the effort in the lat area. Pull back to the original position and repeat.

The start of the lat machine pulldown (top) and the finish (bottom) as performed by Bob Jodkiewicz.

Lat-Machine Pulldowns

This exercise has to be performed on a lat-machine. Take a wide overgrip on the bar and pull down as far as you can. This exercise is not as effective as the wide-grip chinning exercise, but does have the advantage that you can use less resistance, and, consequently, can pull the bar lower and work your lats over a greater range of movement.

Rocky DeFerro performs low pulley single arm rowing.

Low Pulley Single-Arm Rowing

Grab hold of the handle of a low-weight pulley and set yourself in a comfortable bent-over position. Starting with the arm straight, pull the handle strongly into the waist. Make the lats feel the effort strongly. Return to arm-straight position and repeat.

Low Pulley Rowing

Perform this movement with a long cable machine. Secure your feet against the apparatus and pull the cable handles horizontally into your midsection. Hold for a second and slowly allow your arms to straighten and ultimately stretch your lats. Pull in again and repeat. You may also perform this exercise on a high pulley.

Jack Niehausen urges Tony Pearson on in the long pulley rowing exercise.

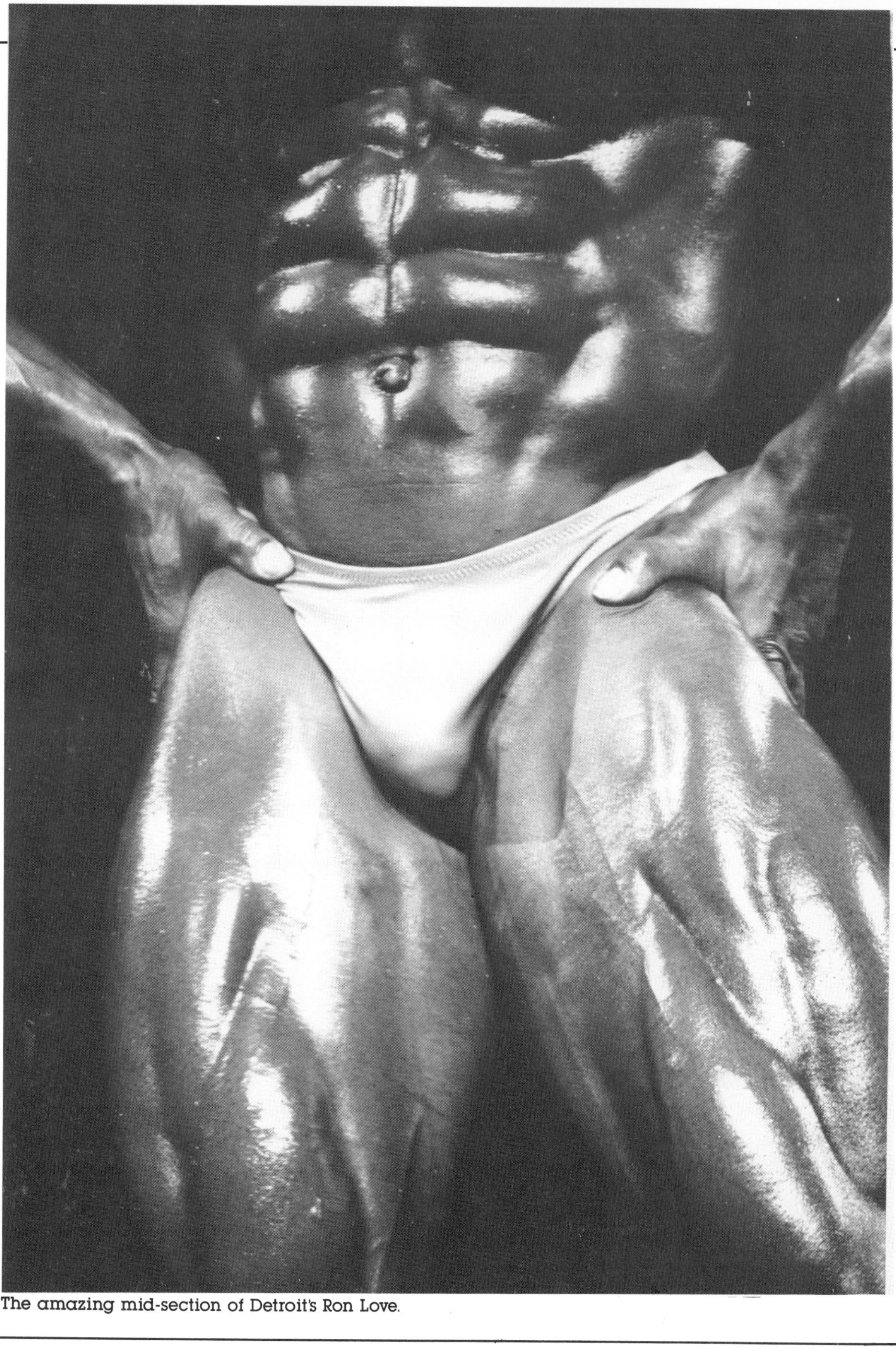

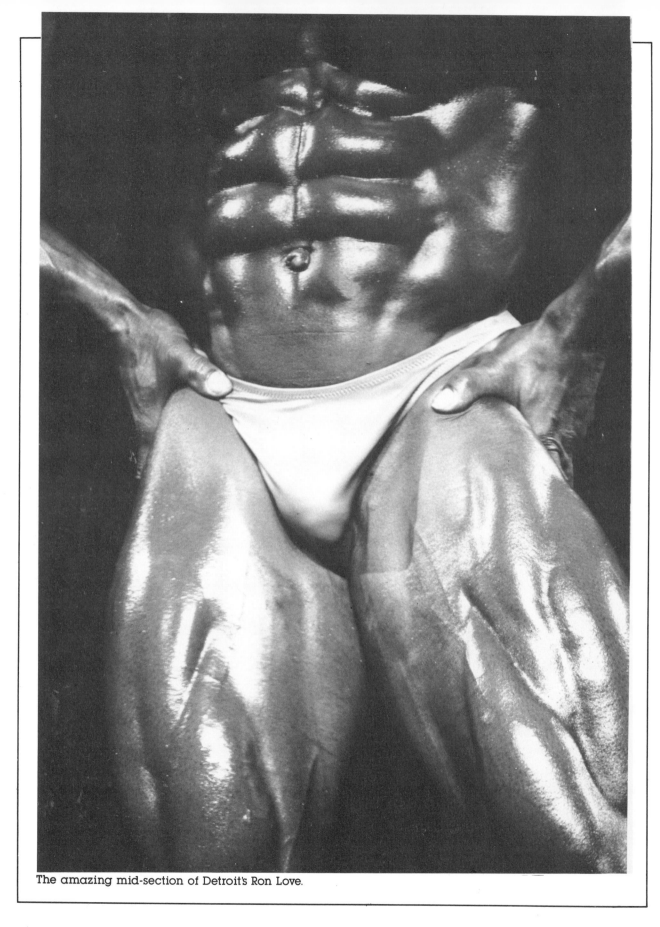

The amazing mid-section of Detroit's Ron Love.

CHAPTER 14
ABDOMINALS

Who wants rock-hard rippling abdominals and a fat-free midsection? Everyone wants them, and, curiously enough, very few people have them. Most of us have midsections that are covered with a thick layer of adipose tissue (fat) and not a few of us have more than just a covering of fat.

Probably one of the most common questions I'm asked is, "How can I get well defined abdominals that are hard and that show up with ridges?" The questioner often is also bothered by fat around the lower back commonly known as "love handles." The answer is twofold: you must exercise the area vigorously two or three times a week at least, and you must also watch food intake, because too many calories will sabotage your efforts to reduce your waistline. For an older person whose metabolism may have slowed down somewhat, obtaining and maintaining good abdominal definition is a hefty undertaking. Although the exercises we perform are important, by far the most essential way to attack any waistline problem is to reduce overall calories. Doughnuts and coffees, cookies and candies, soft drinks, pizza are not the way to a slender waistline.

Few people have abdominals that are spread in even rows across the waistline. Those who come to mind that do have evenly lined-up abs include Mohamed Makkawy, Dennis Tinerino, Samir Bannout, Franco Santoriello, Laura Creavalle, Bob Paris, Berry DeMey, Gary Strydom, and Rich Gaspari. Unfortunately, no amount of exercise will change the placement of your abdominal muscles. If they are uneven now, then that is how they will stay for life. Vigorous exercising will not line them up so that they form perfectly straight rows.

Actually it is doubtful if any physique judge would deduct points for a person who failed to show a straight line of abdominals. The main criterion for judging the midsection is that they be sharply defined, and show up as bricks in the waistline area.

It is commonly accepted that if you perform 20 to 30 repetitions of situps and leg raises each night before going to bed that you would develop an impressive tight waistline. This is just not true. Regular abdominal exercise will firm up the tummy muscles, but it is seldom enough to make them show up as ridges, because the small amount of exercise that one does, to give tone to the area, is not sufficient to burn off the excess weight that accumulates around the waistline. It is, therefore, often necessary to combine a system of aerobics with a special calorie-reduced diet. Don't look for immediate results because even small amounts of fat covering the abdominal region can be difficult to immobilize, simply because the waistline is one of the last areas to lose fat. Sometimes one needs several months of hard dieting to get the abdominal ridges to show impressively.

How do we train the abs? Should we perform very high repetitions as men such as Bill Pearl, Irving Kozewski, and Eddie Giuliani do, or should we merely perform sets of normal repetitions? Eddie Giulianni who is one of the principal trainers in World Gym, Venice Beach, still exercises his abdominals by the clock. He performs 30 to 40 minutes of abdominal exercise each time he trains his midsection. He doesn't count sets or repetitions, he merely exercises according to the clock. In his heyday he never did less than 1,000 repetitions of Roman chair situps and a similar number of leg raises. Vince Gironda, of Vince's Gym, was one of the first to call for reps in moderation. "The abs are just another muscle group. Super-high reps are not needed," says the Iron Guru. Other bodybuilders support the Gironda philosophy. "Twelve to 15 repetitions of abdominal movements are all that is needed."

There's also a school of thought whose philosophy is somewhere between the two extremes. Quite a few modern day bodybuilders believe in performing 100 to 200 reps for abdominals so that the waistline is kept active. Now in his 50's, Serge Nubret still performs an hour's abdominals every time he exercises his waist. Serge has consistently lost one-quarter of a centimeter off his waist every year for the last 10 years.

If you haven't been training your waistline for some time, get back into your exercises slowly because the abdominal area is very sensitive. It houses the central nervous system for the body, and if you overwork the area, you could put the rest of your physique into a form of shock whereby it would stop growing. This is the last thing you need as an aspiring bodybuilder.

My own thoughts run to performing moderately high repetitions for abs, about 15 to 50 per set. You will find out by trial and error what appears to work best for you. However, it is not a good idea to do a great number of abdominal exercises late at night, because a great deal of repetitions could lead to sleeplessness, a condition that is not relished by the hopeful champion.

Few people realize that progressive resistance exercise actually creates edema (bloating). This is the natural result of heavy exercise. The last area that you want bloated is your waistline. Something else that also contributes to a heavy-looking midsection is the ingestion of anabolic steroids. True enough, the abdominals themselves thicken and get harder, but there is also a secondary effect of waistline increase and bloat, which does not help the overall physical aesthetics. This "bloat" is unattractive and judges will mark down those bodybuilders whose waists appear to be hanging out all over the stage.

Because heavy exercise tends to cause at least a modicum of edema it is not a good idea to train for 4 to 5 days prior to a contest. I suggest that the competing bodybuilder spend plenty of time in posing and tightening the muscles during these last few pre-contest days. To work out will only defeat your aim of trying to achieve maximum muscle definition.

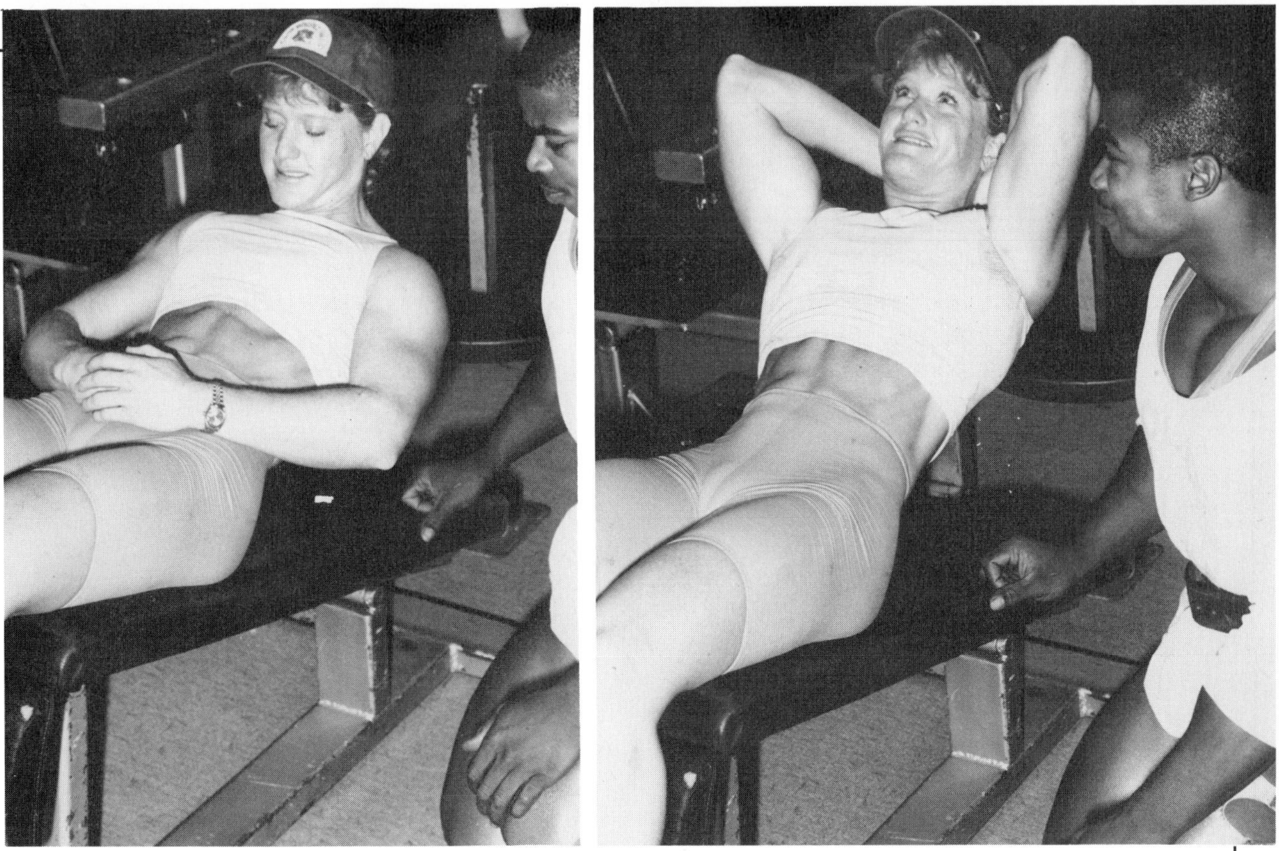

Laura Beaudry starts and finishes the incline twisting sit-up.

There's no better advice to the bodybuilder, whether he or she is a competitive bodybuilder or not, than never to lose control of your waistline.

I have seen many individuals who start training waistlines hard in March, April, or May in the hope that they will have an impressive midsection for the summer activities. Quite often they never quite come into their peak shape at the time when they want it, and the abdominals never manage to surface. Another year is lost. Don't allow your abdominals to stretch out too far. Exercises like squats are not particularly good for the midsection. This is one reason why I advocate a belt for squatting, not just to help the lower back, but to hold in the abdominals, which during the performance of deep-knee bends can be pushed out and overextended. When this happens continually, the midsection becomes overstretched, and this is an irreversible situation. The actual fibres of the abdominal wall are overextended like a spring that's been pulled too far, and they will not click back into place.

Incline Twisting Sit-Ups

Lie back on an incline board set at any angle you prefer (the steeper the angle the lower the part of the waist worked). Your feet should be held to the board with a strap (or bar under which the feet fit). Place your hands behind your head and curl upwards. Keep the knees bent slightly throughout the movement.

Hanging Leg Raise

Hang from an overhead horizontal bar, with your arms about 30 inches apart. Raise your legs until they are just past the parallel to floor position, lower and repeat. Try not to allow the body to build up a swinging motion. This exercise works the very important lower abdominal region, right down into the groin.

For those who are unable to perform this exercise with straight legs, start off with the knees bent. Tuck your knees into the waist in each repetition. Start the raise slowly, with positively no swinging. After a few weeks you will be able to graduate to the straight-leg style.

Marjo Selin assists Tonya Knight in three stages of the hanging leg raise.

Crunches

Lie on your back on the floor. Your calves should rest on a bench in such a way that your thighs are more or less vertical. Place your hands behind your head and attempt to sit up. Because of the position of the legs the peak contraction is not passed over as in the regular sit-up. There is constant tension in the middle and upper abdominals.

Roman Chair Sit-Ups

You need a Roman chair to anchor your legs in position and allow the trunk to sit below parallel, thus working the abdominal region to a great degree. Perform this with a steady rhythm and no bouncing. This is the favorite exercise of Irv "Zabo" Kozewski , who has won more "best abdominals" awards than any other bodybuilder.

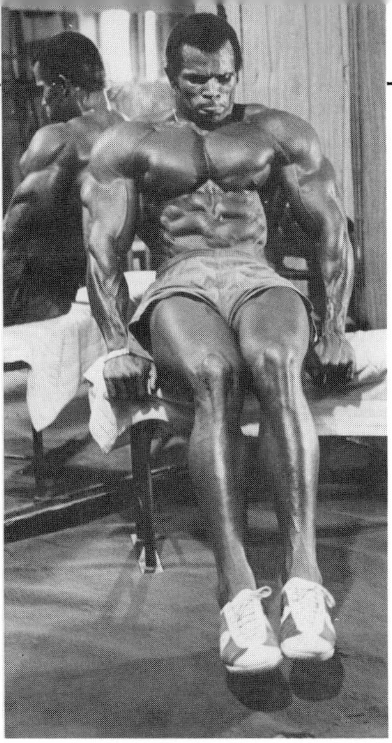

Serge Nubret starts the seated knee-ins (top) and finishes (bottom).

Steve Brisbois performs the lying crunch exercise.

Ed Giuliani and Zabo Kozewski have performed more Roman chair sit-ups than anyone else.

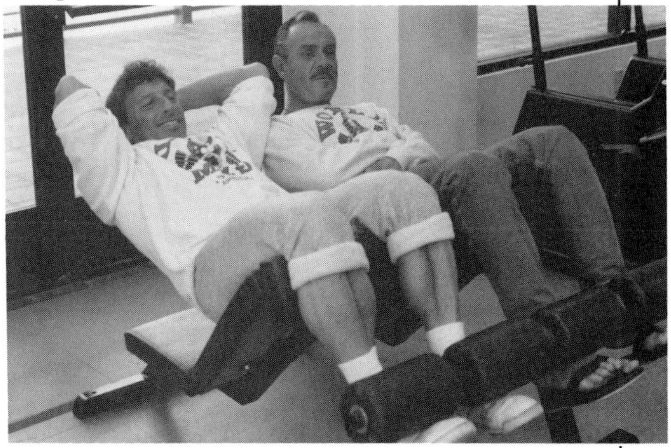

Seated Knee-Ins

This movement trains the lower abdominals. Sit on a bench, gripping the sides for support. Tuck your chin in and lean back at about a 45° angle. Raise the knees to the chest area. Lower, and repeat. Concentrate the effort into the lower abdominals.

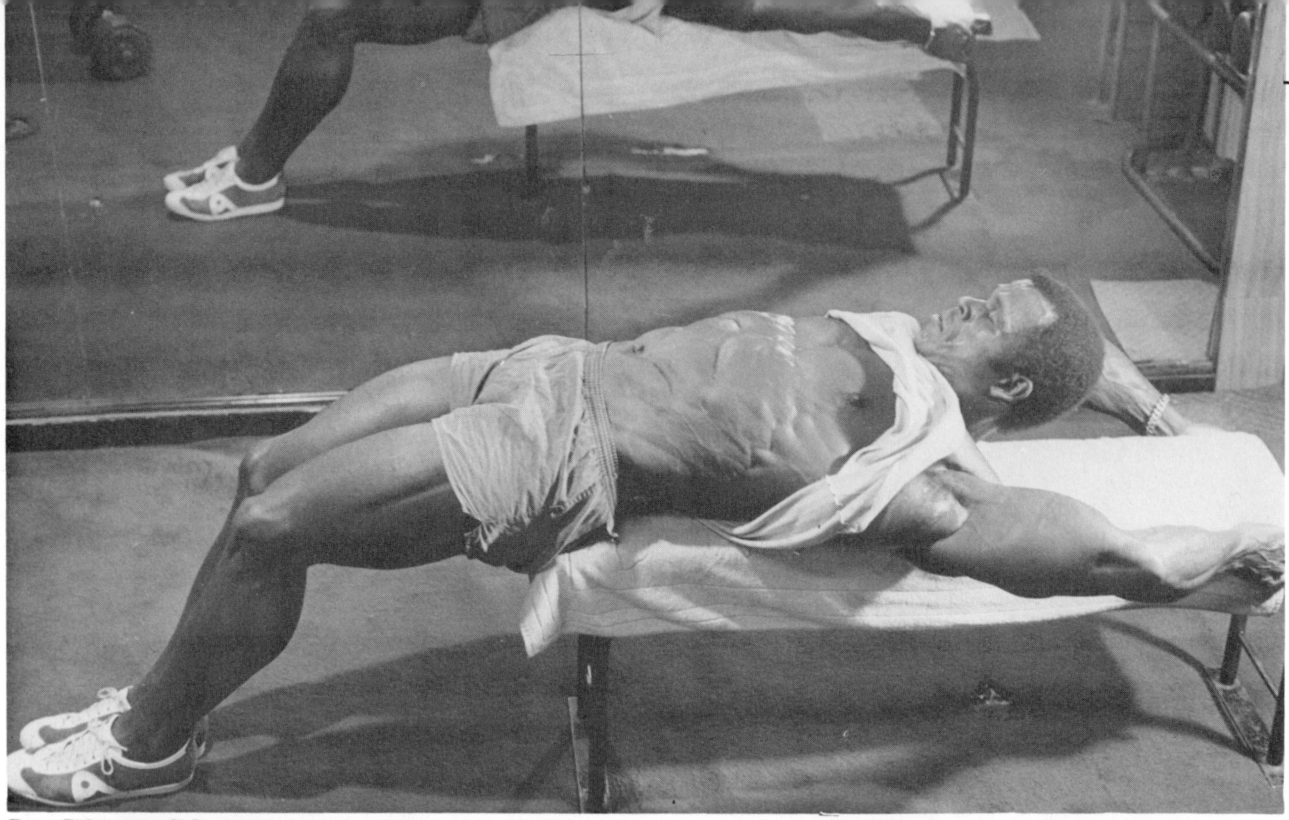

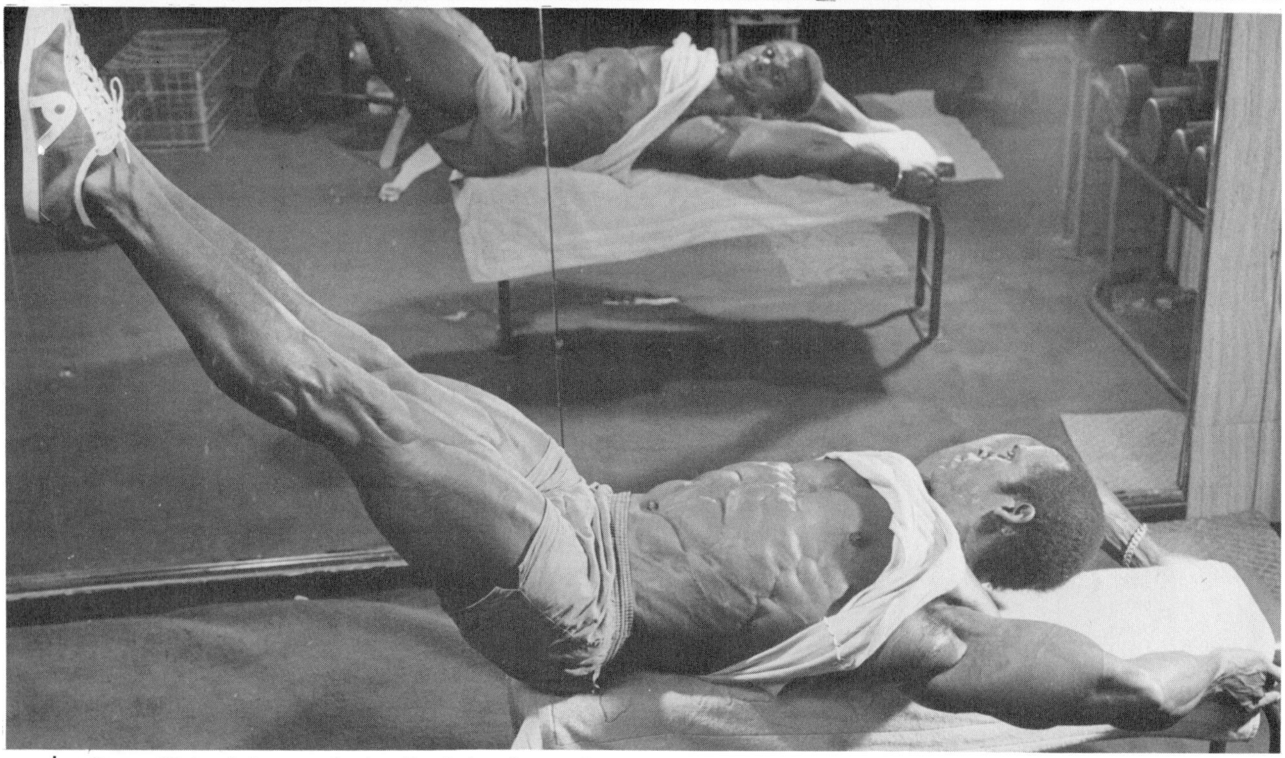

Serge Nubret demonstrates the lying leg raise.

Lying Leg Raise

Lie flat on your back on a standard bench, holding on to the vertical uprights firmly. Keeping your back on the bench, raise your legs up from the ground until vertical. Lower, and repeat. This exercise works the middle and, to an extent, the lower abdominals.

Broomstick twists shown by Serge Nubret.

Broomstick Twists

Not all bodybuilders believe in the efficacy of this exercise. It does, however, mobilize the waist area, and the obliques are worked quite strongly despite little or no resistance. Too, your ability to twist in certain poses will be greatly facilitated. Perform high repetitions as you twist from side to side, and make a conscious effort *not* to turn your hips too much to either side.

Decline dumbbell presses performed by Gunther Kuni work the lower chest line.

Bodybuilders are conversant with numerous techniques, principles, and advancements that many have found helpful in their training. However, there is still a great deal of conjecture as to which principles are best and which hold little value. In your case, I suggest that you, once past the beginner's stage of training, undertake a planned system of experimentation. Try various principles for 4 to 10 weeks to see how they affect your progress. There is no single best system of training, just as there is no single best combination of sets and repetitions. Bodybuilding is an ongoing experience. Once past the beginner's stage you should undertake to experiment in a planned sequence to find out which systems work best for you. It is the variety of training principles that can keep your muscles guessing and growing.

CHAPTER 15 PRINCIPLES AND TECHNIQUES

Following are some of the more workable systems in the sport.

STRAIGHT SETS

This method is the most widely used of all, and arguably it is the most productive method. Straight sets simply means that you perform a set of repetitions in a certain exercise, followed by a rest of a minute or so, and then, a second, third, fourth, or even fifth set is performed on the same exercise with a suitable rest period in between. After several sets of one exercise, you then go over to another exercise and perform several sets of that movement. Frequently, exercises for the same body part are grouped together when one uses the straight sets' system. For example, you would group all the chest exercises together or all lat exercises together, shoulders, biceps, triceps, and so on. Straight sets have been used now for over a century but extensively only after World War II. If there is one system that has built more muscles mass than any other it is the straight-sets system.

FORCED REPS

The technique of forced reps, which has been with us for a long time, was re-introduced in the late '70s by Mr. Heavy Duty, Mike Mentzer. What is a forced rep? It is the forced continuation of an exercise after normal failure has taken place. This is to say, when you can't perform another repetition in the bench press, you can have a training partner place his palms under the bar and help you up with the weight. This can be done, with just enough "lifting help," to enable the exerciser to perform the two or three additional reps that wouldn't normally be possible. It doesn't take a genius to realize that when an exercise is "extended" in this way, that additional muscle fibres are brought into play and that more mass is solicited because of the additional workload and prolonged effort.

In most cases forced reps require a partner to help you—either to raise the bar upwards in exercises like presses, squats, rows, curls, etc., or in the case of chins, to lift your body. Certain apparatus have built-in spotting principles that can be utilized to lighten the load. In some cases, you can do it yourself. For example, when Lee Haney performs the concentration curl and reaches positive failure, he will hold the wrist of his hand with his free hand and gently help the exercising arm raise the weight upward. I first became aware of the technique of forced reps in the '50s. John Carl Grimek, the only two-time Mr. America, observed Steve Reeves's training and wrote:

"Watching Steve Reeves train in the old York gym was both educational and inspiring. Steve performed higher reps than most other stars of the day, and he liked to work his entire body, each workout, training three times a week. Often I would see Steve perform an exercise such as the seated dumbbell curl where he would curl the weight for 10 or 12 repetitions, and when the moment came where he was unable to perform another rep, he would kick the weight up with his foot and lower it slowly, thus taking advantage of the negative side of the exercise. At other times he would cheat-curl a heavy barbell and lower it slowly, as *slowly* as he could."

Today, the forced reps concept has been revived to an extent by modern bodybuilders who use them occasionally, especially in lifts such as the bench press or incline bench press. The use of forced reps throughout workouts for every exercise is not recommended. You would very soon find your body reacting negatively because the constant excessive strain would very likely put your body into a state of shock, and all growth would quickly come to a standstill. We mentioned that Reeves would kick the weight up, and then lower it slowly. Sometimes this is done with a barbell, whereby the weight is thrown up in a loose, cheating style, and then lowered slowly. This doesn't really come under the heading of a forced repetition. It is known today as a negative repetition. Negative reps must be used with caution. For example, if you are able to curl 120 pounds 8 times in strict style, there may be some value to throwing the last 2 or 3 reps up in a loose style and lowering them slowly, so that the negative part of the repetition is felt by the biceps. On the other hand, assuming that you can curl that same 120-pound weight, it would not be a good idea to load up a barbell to 160 or 180 pounds and curl it up in a sloppy, loose style and *then* try and lower it slowly, feeling the negative effect. The difference between what you can curl positively, and what you can lower slowly should not be great. By all means follow this principle for some exercises at the appropriate time, using the appropriate resistance, but do not try and use monumental poundages that the muscles in question will find very difficult to control. You could cause a very serious injury.

SUPERSETS

Supersetting is the use of two different exercises of opposing muscle groups in an alternating fashion. For example, if we are training the upper arms, a good superset would be to work the biceps and the triceps alternatively. That is to say we would perform a set of barbell curls, followed quickly by a set of triceps extensions. The usual way to perform a superset is to alternate two different exercises for 3 to 5 sets each, at which time you have a rest before moving on to another superset or different body part entirely.

Supersetting shouldn't really be done throughout an entire workout. It is a time-saving method which really blitzes an area and can lead to some pretty outstanding results when performed correctly. Remember to always alternate rapidly without rest one pulling movement and one pushing movement. You can work the upper legs by performing a set of thigh curls followed by a set of thigh extensions. Continue this for 4 or 5 sets. Many men and women in bodybuilding today swear by alternating chest and back exercises. They insist that there is a usefulness in performing these supersets. Much is made of the claim that one helps recuperation of the other. Too much supersetting can cause stagnation in progress. However, paradoxically, you can break a sticking point with a few weeks of supersetting some of your exercises.

BI-SETS

A bi-set is similar to a superset but you do not perform exercises of different bodyparts. A bi-set is performing two exercises on the same body part in an alternating manner. For example, you may bi-set two chest exercises, or two thigh exercises, or two biceps exercises, etc. Again, like supersets, the advantage of bi-setting is that you can get a lot of work done in a short period of time, and the method contributes greatly to pumping blood into the area. It is not necessarily a good way of building pure power; however, there is great worth in the effect that comes from concentrated bi-setting.

TRI-SETTING

This method involves performing three exercises for the same muscle group, one after the other, with very limited rest between exercises. You may rest for 90 seconds or so at the conclusion of all three exercises; however, when you perform your second tri-set, perform all three exercises without rest between the movements. A typical tri-set for the chest would be the incline bench press, flat bench press, and the crossover pulley machine. It is often a good idea to hit a particular muscle from three different angles, and the tri-set method is an ideal way.

CHEATING

This method has been used since the earliest workouts because when you cheat you use techniques such as bouncing and swinging and bending and leaning back and jerking to get the weight from A to B. Now we all know that this is a technique of the strongman who has to get the weight from the ground to the arms straight above the head position, but is it also useful for the bodybuilder? Yes, because cheating using loose training style is sufficiently different from performing exercises in the strict manner that it offers a new shock to the muscles.

Today, however, cheating is not done in such a way as to merely lift the weight from A to B. The bodybuilder must use what is known as creative cheating. That is to say, you should rock the weight, lean, twist or whatever, to make the muscles feel more stress, rather than to relieve them from stress as you would when trying to merely lift the weight above the head. For example, if you curl a weight 10 times in a strict pattern and can no longer lift any more, then to involve yourself, in slightly leaning back and thrusting the weight upwards, you can continue with more muscle involvement, especially if you lower the weight in a controlled fashion. Cheating gets us through the sticking point of the strength curve. Again, we may not be able to lift the weight at a certain point of the strength curve, but if we get a little momentum going then we can pass the difficult area and then proceed with the lift through the normal range of motion.

There are certain cheating movements that you should not do. It is definitely not recommended that you bounce up and down in a ballistic fashion, in the squat, for example. This can cause lower back injuries and certainly is far too stressful for the knees. In another way, raising the back while doing bent-over rows for the barbell, or a T-bar apparatus, can also be detrimental to the lower or middle back. A strain or muscle tear could result.

When bench pressing, you may be tempted to cheat by bouncing the bar on the chest, as it is lowered to the sternum. This again is not advised. Bodybuilders have been known to crack the sternum by doing this with excessive weights. Cheating is useful for adding muscle size, but I can't stress enough the importance of being *creative* with your cheating and using loose style to achieve added effect on the muscles, rather than merely using the method so that you can claim to be lifting heavier weights. A bodybuilder should not be training to satisfy the ego. You are training to build muscle size and tone, definition, and separation. Cheat to benefit these aspects and not to feed your ego.

PEAK CONTRACTION

A peak contraction exercise is any exercise where the conclusion of the movement also coincides with the exercise's most difficult point. A typical example would be the bench crunch, where one lies on the floor with the calves resting on a bench, face up, so that the thighs are vertical to the floor. Hands behind head, you then sit up to work the abdominals and at the point where you can come up no more, the exercise is at its most difficult aspect. This is known as peak contraction. Other peak contraction movements include the wide-grip upright row, wide-lat machine pulldowns, triceps kickbacks performed in the bent-over position, standing leg curls, wide-grip bent-over rows, wide-grip chins, 90° preacher bench curls, crunches, gravity boot sit-ups, thigh extensions and incline triceps stretches. There are scores of exercises that can be altered to peak contractions simply by changing the angle of the bench's pulley and weights in relation to the position of your body.

For example, Vince Gironda turns a calf raise into a peak contraction exercise by having his students face the opposite way on a hack machine, holding the side handles while performing heel raises. By using a lat machine and lying under it, in a supine position, you can do a useful peak contraction pulley curl. Few training methods make more use of the mind than peak contraction. You need to have extreme concentration at the conclusion of each repetition, and the maximum number of nerve impulses are being fired off by the muscle. It is often a good idea at this stage to count to one before lowering the weight. In other words you are holding the contraction for about a second before allowing the weight to return to the start position.

Advanced bodybuilders who use peak contraction in some of their exercises agree that the muscles should be tensed deliberately after one reaches the contracted point. In other words, use the principle of isotension, squeeze the muscles, and flex them to their fullest at the conclusion of each peak contraction repetition.

GIANT SETS

Sometimes this advanced musclebuilding technique method is known as compound training. It goes beyond biceps and triceps. In the case of giant sets one groups together four or five exercises for one bodypart and performs one after the other without rest until all four or five exercises have been completed. At that time you may rest for a minute or two and then go on to completing the other giant sets. A typical compound training set for the deltoids would consist of:

Press-behind-neck 10 reps
Seated Alternate Dumbbell Press 12 reps
Wide-grip Upright Rowing 12 reps
Seated Dumbbell Lateral Raise 12 reps
Short Rest

One usually repeats the entire giant set routine two or three times before moving on to another bodypart. It is not suggested that you perform giant sets for your entire routine, although some people have done this with a degree of success. Far better to concentrate on one or two bodyparts by using compound training.

UP AND DOWN THE RACK

If you're lucky enough to have your own full set of dumbbells ranging from a pair of 10-pounders all the way up to 90's, 100, or even more, this system can work wonders for you. Otherwise, you are going to have to use the dumbbell rack at the gym and because of overcrowding the up-and-down-the-rack principle is not always practical. The name explains the method. Any exercise that you usually do standing up with dumbbells can be chosen. Begin with a light pair of dumbbells, for example, for the standing dumbbell press. Perform a given number of repetitions. Don't go to exhaustion, just go to where the last rep is a little stressful. After you perform one set, immediately replace the weights in the rack, and pick up the next heaviest set of dumbbells. Perform between 6 and 10 repetitions with those dumbbells. When you can no longer perform any more, then replace those dumbbells for yet a heavier set and perform another 4 to 6 reps. Go up as high as you can with your pairs of dumbbells until you can only do about 3 repetitions. At this time, start coming down the rack again, using progressively less and less weight. This

Vince Comerford stresses out his upper arms with the barbell curl.

Tom Platz wrestles with the press-down bar to work his triceps to exhaustion.

method is absolutely perfect for hitting the various aspects of the muscle with different varieties of repetition counts. In just one up-and-down-the-rack set you may be performing as few as 3 repetitions and as many as 20.

This method has been used by old-timers Larry Scott and Vince Gironda and is today used by many top stars in the bodybuilding field.

THE STRIPPING METHOD

This is a pretty old technique used for a long time by European bodybuilders. In England it is known as the "Triple Drop." Arnold Schwarzenegger enjoyed and used this method a great deal during his training for the various Mr. Olympia titles that he won. Stripping is best described as the performance of 3 sets in 1. Certainly, you get more out of a single set of stripping than you would out of a normal straight set. It could be argued that a set doesn't really begin to work the muscles until the last 2 or 3 repetitions.

In the case of the stripping method one works the muscles very hard, two or three times during any particular set. Begin a set of bench presses, for example, with a weight in which you can only do about 6 repetitions. Perform your 6 repetitions and when you cannot perform another count, signal to your training partner to take off a 15-pound disc from either end of the bar. This should be done quickly so that there is no loss of time. As soon as the discs are removed continue with your set and perform as many repetitions as you can. Again, as you get to the stage where you cannot do any more, signal again to your training partner to remove yet another disc from either end of the bar. As soon as this has been carried out, continue with further repetitions until the end of the set. As you can see, this method is very severe because we reach the point several times where we can do no more during a single set, whereas in the normal set where no weights are removed we only meet the stress of exertion at the end of the set.

The stripping method can be used on many different exercises such as squats, curls, but it's usually only done in a few exercises per workout. Do not try and perform the stripping method on every exercise every workout, because it is too severe for the body to handle. You would risk the likelihood of body shock syndrome, which would cause you not to gain, but to lose weight.

REST PAUSE

This method is not unlike the triple dropping method in that one reaches several "last reps" during a single set in which the muscles are maximally stimulated. Again, rest/pause is not a system to be followed all the time. It does permit one to greatly increase tendon muscle strength and to add overall muscle mass in a small amount of time.

The idea is relatively simple. After warming up for a particular exercise, load up the barbell sufficiently to allow just one or two repetitions, assuming you are bench pressing. Press out a couple of difficult repetitions and then replace the bar on the stands. Allow 10 to 20 seconds to elapse and perform another couple of repetitions. After a similar brief rest, perform yet another couple, and so on. Actually, you could start out with about 4 repetitions and keep resting and pressing until you can only do one repetition. This is a very severe form of exercise so keep it in moderation, especially if you are not used to this form of excessive intensity.

THE MUSCLE SPINNING ROUTINE

Muscle spinning was a method used as a reaction to heavy weights used by weightlifters and old-time strongmen of the pre-World War II era. Muscle spinning is actually the use of very light weights, while performing high repetitions, in strict style, and in a rhythmic fashion. Muscle spinning is the exact opposite of heavy-duty training. In heavy-duty training, you use low sets and moderate repetitions with absolutely all the weight you can handle. At the conclusion of a set you continue on with forced reps and negative reps so that when the set of heavy-duty repetitions is completed you are totally exhausted. The muscle spinning is a total antithesis of this method in that you will perform 20 to 30 repetitions of each exercise with relatively low intensity. It's a fact that if you use muscle spinning after heavy-duty training you will definitely not notice any new muscle gains for several weeks. You will lose muscle at first because the body is used to the heavier training, and muscle spinning does not translate into more muscle until the body is used to this particular method. After a few weeks, however, you may find that muscle spinning has its uses and a period of eight to twelve weeks can be afforded this method. Today, there are quite a few bodybuilders who perform 90 percent of their workouts utilizing this method. It definitely works for some, but to be fair there are those who have given it a chance only to find that they got no gains whatsoever. Some bodybuilders today perform muscle spinning movements on their off days to pump the blood into the muscle so that the area is kept gorged with blood throughout the so-called rest day after being worked in the more conventional straight sets fashion, training to positive failure.

HEAVY AND LIGHT ROUTINE

Bodybuilders from the past Reg Park and Bill Pearl both used a system of heavy and light training to build their title-winning physiques. In the same workout, they trained with identical muscle groups using both high poundages with low repetitions and low poundages with high repetitions. Today, modern experts agree that there is evidence to show that their reasoning was sound. High reps and low reps give different results and can contribute size to a bodypart that one method alone cannot. Do not confuse light repetitions with wasted loose style repetitions whereby momentum comes into play and thereby reduces muscular contraction. A weight must always be lifted, even when the weight is light, and not thrown. A repetition performed under momentum has little value. The muscles must do the work of lifting the weight whether it's light or heavy.

It is often a good idea to pause momentarily at the top of the contracted position, then to find that contraction mentally, to squeeze it to confirm that it's there, and then and only then lower it to the start position. There are two methods involved with the heavy and light routine:

1. You can perform several sets of an exercise with heavy weights and low reps and then perform some light sets with high reps using the same exercise.

2. Alternatively you can perform a basic multi-joint exercise using heavy weights, and then after several heavy sets, you can change to an isolation exercise and use high reps for 3 or 4 sets. This still takes advantage of using both high and low repetitions in the same workout for the same bodypart.

Cory Everson likes to work her rear deltoids one at a time.

Bodybuilding is no longer for men alone. Women want firm athletic bodies, too. Today, women use free weights and weight machines to shape, build, reduce and tone. And nothing works faster. Women's bodybuilding is well established. Actually there have always been women bodybuilders. *Strength and Health* and *Iron Man* magazines ran features on women bodybuilders as far back as the 1950's. But the modern approach to women's bodybuilding was started by Lisa Lyon who catapulted to fame when a few of her pictures were seen in the muscle magazines around 1975. Lisa exhibited a very muscular appearance and although she was not big as far as muscle mass was concerned, she drew a great deal of adverse reaction. She was regarded as a freak, a bodybuilding curiosity. Scorned by many, Lisa persevered with her bodybuilding and gradually people who originally hated the "new breed" of women, were changed around to the point where they actually admired the feminine muscular look. Appreciation for Lisa mounted when subsequent photos showed her looking feminine.

CHAPTER 16

BODYBUILDING FOR WOMEN

Like Arnold Schwarzenegger before her, Lisa Lyon could lay on the baby oil and crunch into a mighty "most muscular" pose, showing separation and definition with the best, and later turn up at a cocktail party, becoming the focus of attention as the most attractive and intelligent woman in the room. Lisa was the inspiration of thousands of women bodybuilders who endeavored to follow in her footsteps, the most notable of which was the scintillating double Ms. Olympia Rachel McLish. Rachel trained intelligently and built a beautiful physique that ultimately became universally admired. Rachel did television talk shows, films, and TV specials, commercials, and hundreds of seminars and posing exhibitions. She became the most famous woman bodybuilder in the world.

Following Rachel, came the winning physique of Cory Everson. Cory won more Ms. Olympias than anyone in the history of the sport. She had her own TV exercise show and ultimately made a fortune selling her Corinnawear Sports clothing line. A natural athlete, Cory could turn her hand to anything. Her loves were tennis, piano playing, and interior decoration, but in truth she could throw a football, run 5000 meters, swim, jump and bike with the best of them.

Don't be misled by the term bodybuilding—it doesn't necessarily mean "building the body." In fact, many overweights find that it is *body reducing*. You can use weights to build up, reduce, add shape, improve tone, increase strength, and develop fitness and health. The end result is that bodybuilding methods can give you a svelte muscular body that is *outrageously* feminine, curvy and attractive.

But why weight training? For some reason women have tended to be suspicious of using weights to tone and shape their physiques. I think it is an innate fear of becoming too muscular and big. Ironically, training with weights will not make you too big or over-muscled. This condition is brought about by bodybuilders who take testosterone based prescription chemicals. Not advised under any circumstances. The truth is that weight training will condition and shape your body faster than aerobics, yoga, stationary bike riding, stair machines, stretching or treadmills. It cannot be beat.

The beauty of weights is that you can *tailor* the resistance to your condition. If you are painfully thin and weak, you can start by using extremely light weights so that you ease yourself into condition as the weeks go by. As you get stronger and fill out, you will be able to add a little more weight to the bar. Gradually, you will bring yourself up to the kind of shape and condition you've always wanted.

Larger or more athletic women may be able to start with slightly heavier weights, but even so, as a beginner to weight training, you should be prepared to start out "light." There is little sense trying to see how much you can lift when you first get into bodybuilding. This can lead to pulled muscles or minor strains, and, ultimately, missed workouts, dejection, and confusion.

Remember *you* are in charge of the weights. *You* are using them as tools to sculpt *your* body to physical perfection. The moment you start trying to lift huge barbells that prove too much for your present strength, you have lost control. The weight is boss instead of you.

Once "into" training, a woman can train as hard as a man. In fact, Vince Gironda observed at his gym in North Hollywood that women often train *harder* than men. "They're wonderful!" Vince exclaimed, "I enjoy them because they show the men what it's all about. They have a higher pain threshold, train stricter, harder and when it comes to displaying their muscles they are better posers."

Women can train using the same exercises as men do. But because they are usually not aiming for maximum size as are the men, they need not perform a huge amount of sets to fully pump the muscles. Three sets per exercise is sufficient.

Bear in mind that your food intake controls both your muscle size and fat content. You can reduce overall size by cutting calories. First the fat will go, then the muscle size itself will diminish if calories are greatly limited. Alternatively, muscle size will increase (if you are training hard) when food intake is increased, and naturally a regular oversupply of calories will result in fat accumulation, which is seldom if ever desirable.

Some women bodybuilders could be said to overdo the degree of muscularity they achieve. At a certain point, if all fat reserves are depleted, the woman bodybuilder will cease to have normal periods (they may stop altogether) and the bust area will reduce significantly. Low fat levels at time of competition are advantageous; however, it is not a good idea to aim for body fat levels below 8 percent. Although some men have reported getting their body fat levels as low as 2.4 percent, women constitutionally have a higher fat percentage than men and should not aim to equal the levels obtained by their male counterparts.

Never be tempted to take any fat-reducing drugs such as thyroid or amphetamines. They will put you in the hospital faster than anything and possibly give *permanent* side effects.

Your first workout is important in more ways than one. Since weight training is the most concentrated form of exercise known, I can't stress too strongly that your first few workouts should be performed with very light resistance. Unless you are naturally strong, well-conditioned and superbly fit right now, use *only* the bar for your first workout. Later as you gain strength, you will add some discs to increase resistance.

SETS AND REPS

To recap, "reps" (repetitions) are the number of times you perform a particular exercise. If you lift a weight up and down 10 times, that is known as 10 repetitions.

A "set" is one *group of repetitions*. As an example, if you did 10 squats, that is known as 1 set of 10 reps (usually written 1 × 10). If you do another group (set) of squats, this is known as 2 sets of 10 reps (written 2 × 10).

Beginners should do *only* 1 set per exercise. In two weeks this can be increased to 2 sets per exercise. In four weeks one can graduate to 3 sets. There is seldom any need to perform more than 3 sets of any exercise, unless you are training for competition.

Repetitions are most effective in the 8 to 12 range. Some women will find they get more from fewer repetitions (6 to 8) while others may prefer performing more (15 to 30). For those completely in the dark about how many repetitions to do, I advise 10–12 reps but you may use up to 30 reps when working the waistline or legs.

EXERCISE PERFORMANCE

When you lift a weight, the movement should always be smooth and rhythmic. There is no value in struggling with the barbell, leaning backwards to "hoist" it overhead, or bending your knees to jerk it into position. Fluid movement, exercise without excessive strain is what is needed. Try to raise the weight rhythmically at the same speed that you lower it: up-down, up-down.

Another "must" whenever you lift: be sure you perform the exercise through its entire range of movement. Whenever you bend your arms during an arm, shoulder or chest exercise, make sure your arms are always straightened (locked-out) during each repetition. With leg exercises, lock-out on each extension. In this way, you will always involve your muscles to their fullest and ensure total flexibility.

BREATHING

Proper breathing during your exercise is important. Try to breath between repetitions. Usually a gulp of air is taken just before the *hardest* part of the movement, and released just as the repetition is *completed*. Try not to hold your breath for any length of time while training. Except in a few nonstrenuous movements, you should breathe once with each repetition, a quick gulp of air through the mouth, exhaling through pursed lips. Unlike in some calisthenics, you should *not* breathe through the nose during weight-training exercise. There isn't time.

REST PERIODS

After each set of exercises you should take a rest. Either take a brief walk around your exercise area or simply stand still. Sitting down is permissible, but not particularly recommended. In the early stages of training, rest for two minutes between sets of exercises. As you gain strength and stamina, try to reduce your rest period. Aim ultimately to rest only one minute between sets. As a general guide, you should rest long enough for your breathing rate to return to normal.

CONCENTRATION

Few things help you more than concentration. Keep your mind on your exercises, and results will come quickly. When you are exercising, you should watch yourself in a mirror to keep an eye on your form and control. With practice you can learn to shut out distraction. Don't carry on a running conversation while training. Keep your mind on what you are doing. You will ultimately be in a world of your own during the time you devote to each set. If a bomb went off behind your back, you should hardly notice it.

WHEN TO INCREASE THE WEIGHT

Beginners often puzzle over when to increase the weight resistance. Add more weight when the resistance you are using feels too light. Weight training should be pleasurable. You will continually have to increase the resistance as you get stronger, but *not* to the extent of making each exercise an all-out superhuman effort. Train, don't strain. When you can easily do 4 or 5 more repetitions than you have planned for a particular movement, that is the time to increase the resistance. You seldom will need to add more than a couple of 2½-pound discs at a time.

BARBELL COLLARS

Don't train without making sure that your weights are secure. Always use collars tightly fastened onto all barbells and dumbbells. The last thing you want is a 5-pound disc slipping from the bar onto your big toe.

HOW LONG SHOULD A WORKOUT BE?

Workouts vary in length from one person to another. At first, while you are getting used to performing each exercise, your workout will be longer, maybe 30 minutes or so. Soon you will be able to cut it down to 15 minutes, maybe less. If you really "get into" weights and have a yearning to reach a peak for a beauty contest, or even a specific photo session, then you may want to add a few extra movements which inevitably increase your workout time. However, don't make the common mistake of thinking that more exercises or more sets will necessarily increase the effectiveness of your training. Each person has a different tolerance for weights. What one woman will find only adequate, another will find too demanding. You must not overwork to the point that you feel overtired and drained the next day. Too much exercise is worse than none. If you overtrain, you will become listless and bored, and will probably end up wanting to forget the whole thing.

EXERCISES FOR BEGINNERS

Every workout should begin with a general warmup period. This can take the form of a 2-minute run, 4 minutes on an exercise bicycle, or a minute spent rope jumping or running in place. The choice is yours, but don't neglect it. Not only does a warmup prepare your muscles for their workout, but it will also make you *feel* like training. It is also important to include the stretches described in the "Warming Up" chapter of this book.

I have selected 20 exercises to show you the

basics of weight training. To reiterate: A beginner should select only one exercise per bodypart and perform this 1 set only, using only a light-to-moderate weight to start with. You can always add extra discs as your muscles get used to the exercises.

As you advance, you can perform 2 or even 3 sets of each exercise, depending on your age, personal endurance and recuperative level. Ultimately, you may even want to add a second exercise for some of your "weaker" bodyparts. Remember though, weight training is an extremely concentrated form of exercise and more is not necessarily *better*. It is far preferable to undertrain than to overtrain.

Seated Dumbbell Press (Shoulders and Arms)

Hold a pair of light dumbbells, 5 to 10 pounds to start, at the shoulders while sitting upright on the end of an exercise bench. Press the dumbbells together to the arms-straight-overhead position and repeat. Breathe in just prior to pressing upwards. Exhale as the arms straighten.

With the use of the dumbbells, each arm is disciplined to work independently. The art of balancing both dumbbells simultaneously may seem difficult at first, but after a few workouts there will be no problem. If you perform this exercise with the elbows held back most of the work is done by the side deltoids. Perform it with the elbows pointing forward and you will bring the frontal deltoids into play. Do 10 to 12 reps.

Upright Rowing (Shoulders and Arms)

Hold a barbell hanging down at arm's length, hands about 8 inches apart. Raise the barbell upwards, keeping elbows as high as possible throughout the movement. Lower under control and repeat. Breathe in before starting to raise the weight; exhale as the bar is lowered. Start with about a 20- to 25-pound barbell. Go for 12 reps.

The start (top) of the seated dumbbell press and the finish (bottom).

The upright rowing movement.

The squat start (top) and finish (bottom).

Squat (Thighs)

The regular barbell squat is like the free-standing squat with the addition of a loaded barbell across the back of your shoulders. If you are very underweight you may want to wrap a towel around the bar where it rests on the upper back to prevent chafing your skin. It is important to keep your head up and your back flat during the entire movement. Starting poundages vary from 30 to 50 pounds, depending on your present strength and condition. Many women bodybuilders are able to squat with double their body weight.

Lower slowly into the squat position keeping the thighs parallel to the floor. Rise slowly to the original upright stance (Illus. 204). At no time should you drop down into a squat and *bounce* up again. The weight must be under control at all times. Start with about 20 to 30 pounds, and 12 to 15 reps.

Hack Slide Squats (Thighs and Hips)

You need a hack slide apparatus for this excellent exercise. Start as shown. Lower into the squat position and immediately rise up. Use only a light weight at first until your body gets used to the movement. Perform 12 to 20 repetitions. Breathe in just before dipping down, exhale as the legs straighten.

Leg Extensions (Upper Legs)

This exercise is done on a special apparatus called a leg-extension machine. A somewhat watered-down version can be done using a table (or high bench) and a pair of iron boots. Using resistance that is comfortable (about 20 pounds), start in the position shown and progress to the legs-straight attitude. Results from this exercise are more often seen in increased definition and shape rather than size. Try 12 to 15 reps and start the lift slowly. Do not "kick" up vigorously because you will be using momentum rather than muscle action to raise the weight.

The start of the hack slide squat (top) and the end (bottom).

The start of the upper leg extension (top) and the end (bottom).

Incline Flyes (Upper Chest)

Start with 10- to 15-pound dumbbells held in the position shown. Arms are slightly bent throughout the exercise to keep strain off the elbow region. Lower the weights, and return to original position. This exercise mainly builds the pectoral area, especially the outer pecs. Do 10 to 12 reps. As in the bench press, it is a good idea to breathe deeply during the exercise (inhale on the way down, exhale on the way up). This has the long-range effect of aiding the rib-cage development.

Bench Press (Chest and Arms)

It doesn't take a genius to see that the bench press movement is in fact an upside-down floor dip. But it is superior as a chest-building exercise because you do not have to hold your body straight nor do you have to balance to the same extent. The most important advantage is that you can add small amounts of weight to the bar on a regular basis. Before you know it you'll be handling respectable poundage in this exercise. Start with 20 to 40 pounds, and be prepared to handle 100 pounds or more within your first year of training. Inhale as you lower the weight, exhale as it goes up. (Imagine you are blowing it up.) Most people lower the weight to the nipple area, but those who wish to build "higher" pectorals may lower the bar to the upper chest. Under no circumstances allow the weight to bounce from the sternum (chest bone) as this could damage the delicate nerve center located beneath it.

When bench-pressing, grip so that the forearms are vertical when the bar is resting on the chest. Push the weight up to arm's length. Do not allow the weight to drop, but rather lower it with control to the original position. Perform between 10 to 12 reps.

The beginning of the incline flyes (above) and the finish (right).

The bench press start (above) and finish (right).

At the top is the start of the lat machine pulldowns and at the bottom is the finish.

Lat Machine Pull-Downs (Upper Back and Arms)

Hold an overhead lat bar using a fairly wide grip. Start with the arms straight and pull the bar down to behind the neck. Return and repeat. Breathe in just before pulling down and release the air slowly as the arms straighten again. Use enough weight to allow for 12 repetitions without undue strain.

Bent-Over Rows (Upper Back and Arms)

Set the body into the position shown, keeping the back flat and the knees slightly bent. Holding a barbell with an overgrip as shown, take a grip width a little wider than shoulder-width. The second part of the movement involves pulling the barbell to the chest. (Begin with about 20 to 30 pounds.) Inhale before lifting, exhale as the weight is lowered. The movement works the entire upper-back and lat area. Do 10 to 12 repetitions.

Leg Curls (Leg Biceps)

Again using the leg-extension machine but this time lying on your front, work the leg biceps through its complete range. Raise the weight from the legs-straight to legs-curled position. Try 12 to 15 reps with 10 to 20 pounds on the apparatus. Inhale and exhale as you feel necessary.

Triceps Extensions (Upper Arms)

Hold a 5-pound dumbbell in the bent-over position. The action of the exercise involves the simple extension of the arm. Breathe as you feel the need; the exercise is not demanding enough to merit deep breathing for every repetition. Do 10 to 12 repetitions.

The bent-over row start (left) and finish (right).

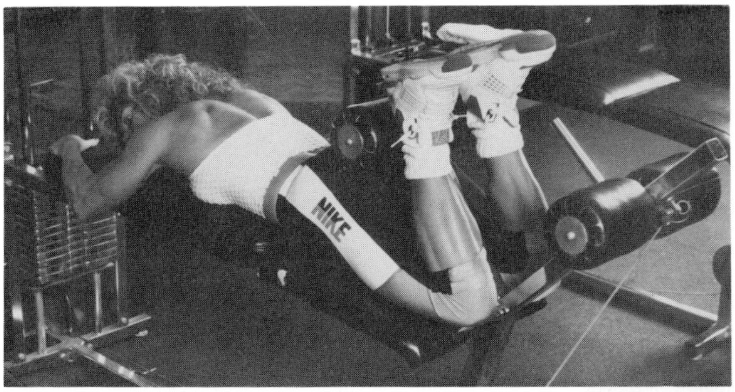

Leg curls on the leg-extension machine. The start is above and the finish at the right.

The triceps extension (the start above, the finish below).

Triceps Pressdowns (Upper Arms)

This exercise can be done only on a special pulley machine. The short bar is held as shown. Keep the elbows tight into the body and the feet comfortably apart on the floor. Take a deep breath and push the bar downwards against the up-pulling resistance. Allow the weight to slowly pull the forearms up again and repeat the effort 10 to 12 times. Exhale each time as the arms straighten. This is one of the best triceps exercises.

Incline Dumbbell Curl (Upper Arms)

Lying back on a 45° incline bench, start your curl with straight arms (15-pound dumbbells are suggested). Inhale as you commence the action, exhale as the arms arrive at the shoulders. Lower at the same speed at which you lifted. Do not permit a "swing" to develop; this takes away from the action. Try 12 reps of this exercise.

Seated Heel Raise (Calves)

This is an advanced exercise usually performed on a special seated calf machine. An alternative is to have someone place a heavy barbell across your knees (make sure you have padding). Move up and down, using about 50 pounds of resistance. This exercise builds shape in the *soleus* area of the calf. Go for 20 reps.

Prone Hyperextension (Lower Back)

Lie face down across an exercise bench. Have a partner hold your legs in place. Start in position shown and rise up into the second position. Lower and repeat. Perform 12 repetitions. This exercise may also be performed on a special padded bench known as a hyper-extension unit.

The triceps pressdown start (above) and finish (below).

The start of the incline dumbbell curl (above) and the finish (below).

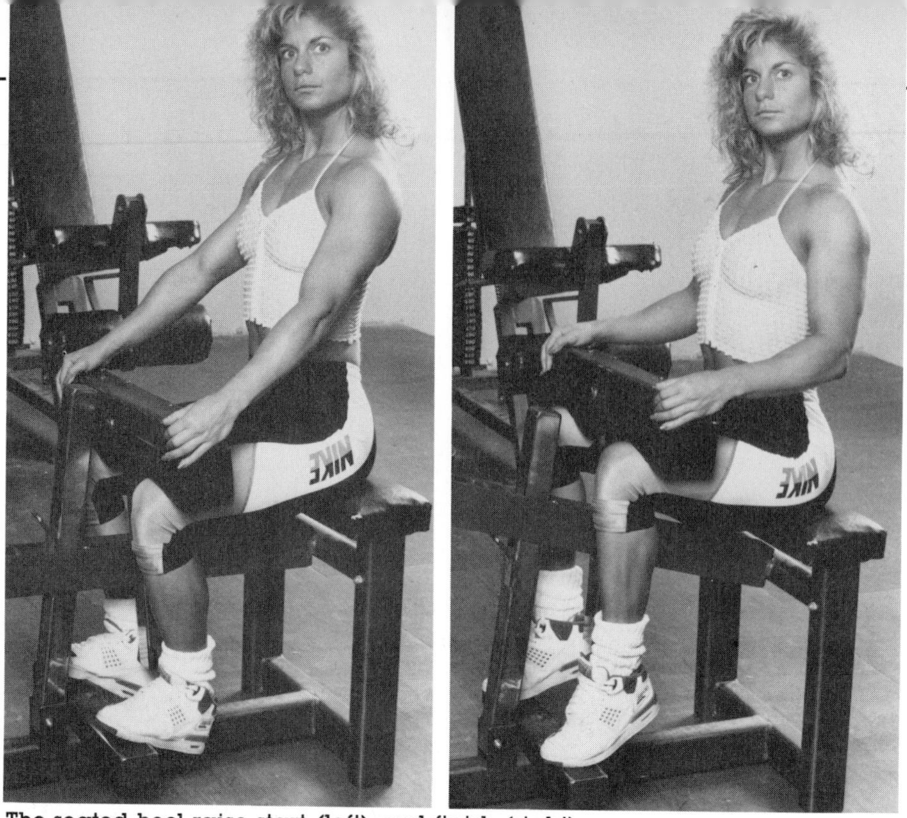

The seated heel raise start (left) and finish (right).

The prone hyperextension start (left) and finish (right).

Roman Chair Sit-Ups (Abdominals)

Use a Roman chair apparatus as shown, and lower your torso slowly back. Rise up and repeat. Ten repetitions are sufficient to start. Work up until you can perform 2 or 3 sets of 25 reps.

"Good Morning" Exercise (Lower Back)

Start with a light (20-pound) barbell across the upper back as shown. Keeping the back flat, and holding strongly onto the bar to keep it in position, lower into the second position. Inhale before going down, exhale as the torso returns to vertical. Try 12 repetitions. This exercise trains the important lower-lumbar region and has a beneficial effect on the legs, especially the hamstring area at the back of the knees.

Calf Raise (Calves)

This exercise also involves the simple process of rising up on your toes (lifting the heels). The resistance can be supplied by a special apparatus (a standing calf machine) or a heavy barbell across the shoulders. Again, use a block under the toes and rise up as high as possible. S-T-R-E-T-C-H. Go for 20 to 25 reps with a 50-pound barbell or use similar resistance on a special calf machine.

Hanging Leg Raise (Lower Abdominals)

This works that hard-to-get-at lower abdominal area. You'll need a horizontal bar (or doorway chin bar) for this one. In summer a tree branch can prove adequate. Start by hanging as shown. Now, with a short breath, inhale and lift the knees. Exhale, lower slowly, and repeat. Try 10 repetitions at first and work up over the weeks until you can perform 30.

Barbell Curls (Upper Arms)

Stand with legs comfortably apart, holding a barbell loaded to about 20 to 30 pounds. Your grip should be about shoulder width or perhaps slightly wider. Without leaning back, take a deep breath and curl the barbell to the shoulders. Do not bend the knees; try to raise the weight while keeping your elbows fairly close to your body. Exhale as the bar arrives at your shoulder level, lower at the same speed at which you raised it and repeat. Try for 12 repetitions. This is the most basic of all biceps exercises and the best one for shaping up that muscle.

The Roman chair apparatus is used for the sit-ups.

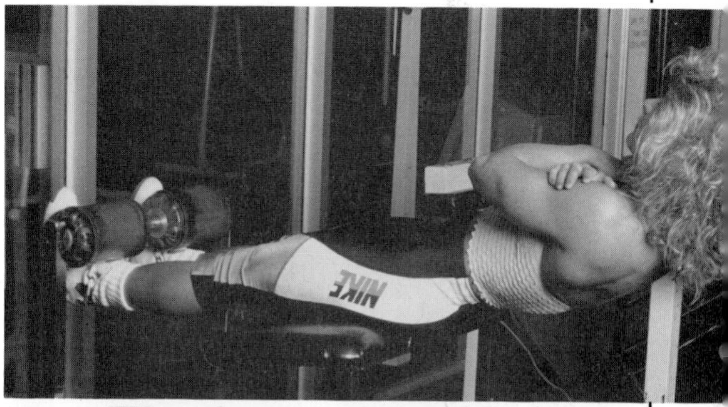

The start of the "good morning" exercise (above) and the conclusion (below).

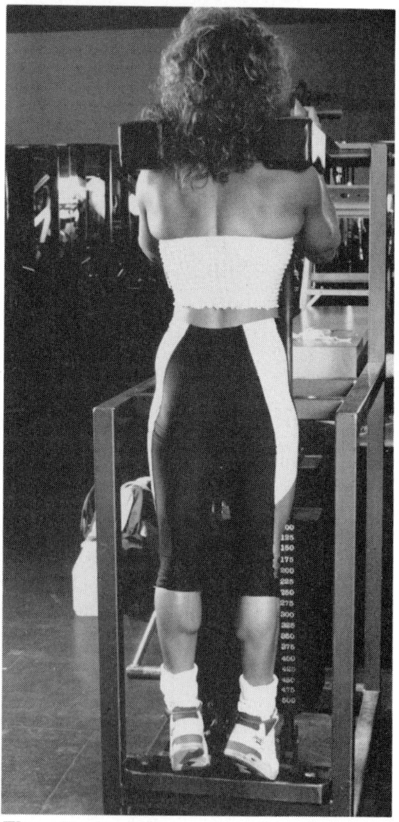

The start of the calf raise (top) and the finish (bottom).

The beginning of the hanging leg raise (top) and the end (bottom).

The start of the barbell curl (top) and the finish (bottom).

Rich Gaspari in a dramatic pose.

CHAPTER 17

THE ART AND DRAMA OF POSING

Much of this book deals with how to build your body. This chapter concerns improving your ability to show off the body you have built! Posing is an essential part of competitive bodybuilding. It is important that you know how to show off your muscles to advantage. This means that not only should you be able to clearly demonstrate to the judges that you have built a proportionate, awe-inspiring body, but also that you are able to display it artistically to music so that you leave the feeling with the audience and judges that you are totally in control of the movement necessary to display your physical prowess.

"Posing is the heart of this thing. Depending on how it's done, you can see in it either everything that is moving and beautiful and dignified about the display of a developed body, or everything that is ridiculous and embarrassing about it." That was a quote from Charles Gaines in his excellent book, *Pumping Iron*.

Although the prime reason for posing is to show others what we've got, there are also side benefits, not least of which are the added muscular size and shape and definition that comes from flexing our muscles. There's no doubt that the flexing of our limbs and tightening of our muscles develops cuts and striations that would not come through normal progressive resistance exercise.

Back at the turn of the century, Eugen Sandow was one of our first famous bodybuilders and the first man to bring us a complete posing routine. He would do this in a glass case on stage known as a posing booth. It was specially lit and he would cover his already white skin with powdered chalk so that the lighting made him look more impressive. Of course, things have changed today. Bodybuilders now seek to be as dark as possible, believing that deep coloration shows off the physique best. After Sandow came Sig Klein and Tony Sanson, both of New York City, and each in his own right a superb poser. Next was John Carl Grimek of York, Pennsylvania, the Monarch of Muscledom. Grimek did not quite have the cuts of today's bodybuilders, but he could really pose, and he had the size and the tan to make him outstanding. His routine, which he performed mainly during the 40's and 50's, was recognized as a complete work of art. Rumor has it that Grimek had a woman friend who was an accomplished ballerina and he learned much about the art of physical display from her. True or not, Grimek was a master.

One incident which lent authority to his reputation as being probably the greatest poser of his time happened at the Mr. Universe contest in London, England, way back in 1948. Steve Reeves had also entered this contest, and you couldn't have picked two more different physical types. Grimek was relatively short at 5′9″. He had a very compact physique with huge, melon-size shoulders, enormous thighs, a thick barrel chest and large 19-inch arms. He contrasted to the equally bronzed Steve Reeves, standing over 6′ tall, with wide rangy shoulders. Lacking Grimek's eye-popping density throughout his entire physique, Reeves somehow made amends with his superb line and beautiful proportions. He was an extremely handsome man, and all his muscles had a contour of unquestionable beauty and masculine grace. He was also extremely defined. Of course, there were other people in this contest, but none of them had the magic physique of these two Americans. It came down in the end to Grimek and Reeves having to pose-off because the judges were unable to select a clear winner. The decision was deadlocked and it was decreed that both Reeves and Grimek should pose once more for the judges.

First Reeves, with his masculine beauty and almost unreal proportions, went through his entire repertoire to the foot-stomping applause of the London audience. It seemed that no one could beat him that day, until, that is, John Grimek stepped up onto the posing platform. What followed made bodybuilding history. Grimek performed an entirely different routine from what he had done previously. This showed that he had an enormous, almost unlimited, repertoire of poses ready to unleash on any audience. Ultimately, Grimek back-flipped off the rostrum, and tossed himself to the ground in full splits. Pandemonium reigned. Applause and cheers battered against the walls and the roof of the theatre and poured in wave after wave towards the now victorious John Carl Grimek. It was one of those moments in bodybuilding that will not be forgotten.

Britisher Reg Park, on leave from the Army at the time, was present at this contest. It was during the Grimek-Reeves posedown that Park decided that he too would one day be a champion. And a champion he most certainly was. Reg was the first person to pose to music at a bodybuilding contest. He chose the perennial strains of "Legend of the Glass Mountain." Reg would perform an arty "stretched-out" stance, and then a "brutal" basic muscle pose, believing that by their contrast each would lend weight and drama to the other. Because of this and what was considered the greatest physique on earth at the time, Reg was in superdemand throughout the world as a guest posing attraction. His fee, outrageous at the time, was £50 ($100). It was of course gladly paid, because Reg Park on the bill virtually guaranteed a full house at showtime. Today, top pro bodybuilders demand anything between $2,000 and $6,000, plus travel expenses, for a five-minute guest spot. After Park came a host of other bodybuilders famous for their inspiring posing ability. These included Chris Dickerson, Frank Zane, Ed Corney, and Mohamed Makkawy. Each man brought to posing a special mixture of art and muscle that made them famous as bodybuilding personalities.

When you enter a contest today you are judged upon several so-called mandatory poses, which include double biceps from the back and front, side chest positions, triceps poses, abdominals, etc. You are also judged in the relaxed position, arms down at the side, from the front, back and sides. At the judging part of the competition bodybuilders will be pulled out in two's and three's so that the judges can compare identical poses. Then there is the free-posing round whereby you walk from the wings to center-stage. Sometimes you have to climb one or two steps to a posing plinth. You position yourself under a spotlight and proceed to perform about 20 poses that show your physique off to advantage. This posing display has to really hit the judges over the head if you are to win the contest.

Your posing routine must incorporate *everything*. That is to say you should show muscle size, proportion, facial confidence, ambition and zest, a complete head-to-toe tan, muscular separation and definition, appealing shape and line, and, of course, artistry and drama in bringing off each and every pose as an aesthetic masterpiece in its own right. After your panic subsides let's analyze each factor.

MUSCLE SIZE

Before entering a contest you should make sure that you've developed an acceptable amount of muscle size, because, after all, you are entering a *bodybuilding* contest. Size is not, however, the most important thing because there are many people who have developed very, very large measurements but because their muscles are not defined and separated these impressive measurements do not show up onstage as being physically attractive. To look good, mass must be accompanied by a low percentage of body fat. The bodybuilder in shape is not necessarily a huge man or woman. In fact you will see more people in the audience who are far bigger than those bodybuilders onstage. But if you were to put those same humungous people in the audience onstage, they would not in all likelihood, look impressive at all. Size has very little to do with how you will appear under stage lights. This is why there is often confusion backstage prior to a contest. Onlookers will notice that one bodybuilder is almost twice the size of another under backstage lighting conditions and, of course, the various finer points of definition can go unnoticed. But it is when the two stand side by side that frequently the smaller bodybuilder totally outshines his larger competitor because of superior shape, definition, separation, or general physique line.

PROPORTION

Entering a contest with poor body proportion or lack of symmetry, if you like, is asking for trouble. Often you will see bodybuilders at contests with poor back development, or underdeveloped calves, or narrow shoulders. These faults become very obvious to the observers, especially the judges who are trained to notice any underpar area.

Have you noticed how cruel bodybuilders can be when they talk of their fellow competitors? I remember that when Arnold Schwarzenegger first came over to the States, he weighed about 240, and he entered the Mr. Universe contest in Miami, Florida, a contest which Frank Zane had entered. The result of this event was that Zane, who was far more proportionate and ripped, was pronounced the winner. Arnold was devastated, because he was on a run of success at the time, and was being touted as the world's greatest bodybuilder. However, he wasn't in top shape for this show, and Zane was. Accordingly, the judges gave Zane the title. Anyway, the cruelty I'm talking about came from Schwarzenegger who complained to his friends that he was beaten by a man who had "no body at all," and this is the way bodybuilders talk of each other. For example, underdeveloped thighs or poorly developed chests

Frank Zane.

often solicit such remarks from other bodybuilders as, "You've got no legs," or "He has no chest at all." This in spite of the fact that you may have 26-inch thighs and a 50-inch chest. Incidentally, Zane equalled the Austrian's insult by commenting after learning of Schwarzenegger's remark that, "Arnold had nothing below the pecs . . . nothing!"

FACIAL CONFIDENCE

This a is very important aspect while presenting yourself onstage. The way you look facially portrays the way you feel about yourself and this presents negative vibrations to the judges who often act accordingly. You must present a confident look in the way you stand and the way you hold your head, and in the actual facial expressions. So often I see contestants with their heads hanging down looking at their chests while they're in the lineup waiting to be called out by the judges. This does not create a positive image. By all means take a quick look down at your chest and abdominals to see that the light has fallen correctly to make them show up but, don't keep looking at yourself as you stand there, looking from one pec to the other, as though your body is going to disappear any second. Once you have checked that the light is correct, then from that moment on, hold your head up high and look confidently out to the audience.

ZEST AND AMBITION

When you're up onstage this is no time to look lacklustre, or disinterested, or nervous. You have to emit a feeling of athletic condition. You must look like a healthy athlete, full of zest and ambition. If you're selling a product, then it has to be done in a positive manner. It has to be seen in the best light and you have to make the request that your potential buyer purchase your product. Onstage as a bodybuilder you are selling yourself—this is no time to be bashful. You now are the salesperson. You have to show everybody that you are serious about winning the contest.

This is probably the one time in your life where you have to feel physically aggressive. You need to assert yourself. Look as though you are prepared to do battle with each and every competitor who is a challenge. You have to dominate the stage. During any posedown comparisons you should be the first to pose and the last to stop posing. You have to show everybody that you are serious about winning the contest. You may well be a nice guy off stage, but onstage when you are called to pose off next to another person then you should become a fighter who never gives in. Of course, the most important time for this type of aggressive posing is during the posedown. Should you be selected as one of the six finalists in a competition you will then be part of the final round which is known as the posedown round. At this time you will have to show every heavy-duty pose in your arsenal. This is no time to perform artistic poses which show ballet-type form and shape. The posedown is when you show maximum muscle and muscularity, and as many heavy-duty poses as you can find time for. Do not hesitate to repeat your best poses in the posedown, and by all means move in closer to other favorites in the competition to show the judges that you are more than willing to be compared. Refuse to quit until the head judge absolutely calls for a cessation of all posing. Wrench every last drop of sweat from your body by refusing to stop posing until your opponents all but collapse in their own pools of sweat.

TANNING

Most bodybuilders use artificial tanning lotions and sunbeds and the natural sun. It's a combination of all three that gives you that golden look. Very few natural tans look even enough when seen onstage, so you will find that the vast majority of bodybuilders also touch up their color with an artificial substance. If you happen to be a black bodybuilder, don't automatically accept the fact that you will look sufficiently tanned onstage. This is a misconception. I have seen bodybuilders in competition from Rick Wayne to Sergio Oliva who have not had sufficient color onstage to look good. I remember remarking once to Danny Padilla after he had looked totally washed out onstage, that he was definitely in need of a suntan. He held his arm up and said, "I can't get any darker. And I'm Puerto Rican." Well, of course, it was just a cop-out because there are many white-skinned bodybuilders who go onstage with superb tans because they've taken the trouble to use artificial substances to give them that all important color. Even very dark skins are enhanced by either artificial tanning lotions, tanning beds, or sunshine. I remember in days gone by Serge Nubret tanning for weeks out in the sun before a contest because he knew the extra edge that came from giving richness to the skin tone. Never rely on just bottle tan alone, especially if your skin is very white. This often gives a green or orange look to the skin. It is far better to get some form of sunlight so that there is a base tone on the body instead of the effect of the tanning lotion. Also with regard to artificial bottle tans, put them on in layers starting about three days before the show, one layer every few hours, until you have approximately ten layers on your skin. This should be done with either a foam brush or a face cloth. You should really experiment with this tanning process on one part of your body, say the thigh or the abdomen, months in advance of a contest. You will then not be taken by surprise by an effect that could take place if you had left it to the end.

I have seen many noticeably bad mistakes with regard to lotions. I once saw a woman come onstage with a totally green look to her because she had applied her tanning lotion incorrectly. Another fellow had worked on the philosophy that tea and oil would give him a good tan for a stage appearance. Apparently he hadn't tried it beforehand and was only going on the advice of another contestant. The result was a terrible mess of streaks that gave a simply dreadful look to the body. This person looked more like a zebra than a human being. It was a pity because he was in a position to pull off a convincing win, but this time around he lost.

If you are going to get your tan from the sun then you need to start a good month in advance of the contest. Few climates can guarantee endless sunny summer days and if you leave your tanning in the sun to the last week you could well find that you only have a couple of days of sun and the rest of the week could be clouds or at best intermittent sunshine. You will then find that you have not got an even tan by the day of the contest. Do not make the mistake, as many people have done, of flying to a warm area to get a sun tan just prior to your contest. Many people have flown to the Bahamas to take advantage of the winter sun, so they come back to the contest really well colored. One guy that I know personally was due to enter the Mr. Canada contest and flew to Las Vegas a couple of days before the show, where he hired a car, drove out to the desert, and lay in the sun for two days solid. He baked himself front, back and sides, and returned to Canada to enter the show, but instead, because of the severe burn that he had acquired, he had to go, not to the contest, but straight into the hospital where he stayed for a week before he recovered.

MUSCULAR SEPARATION

Separation is the clarity of the dividing line between the muscles. That is to say, where the shoulders run into the pectorals there should be a definite line or separation that can be seen. Likewise, with the various muscles of the thigh or the calf or any other group you care to mention. Separation is very important because you can have definition (which is a low percentage of body fat) and yet not have muscle separation. How do you develop separation? This comes from the performance of *isolation* exercises. It also comes about from plenty of posing and practicing the control of the various muscles by squeezing and tightening them as you would during a posing exhibition. Today, a thigh is only a great thigh if it is perfectly defined between the vastus internus and the vastus externus and the sartorius and the various adductor muscles at the top of the thigh. Likewise, of course, today it is important to have separation in all muscle areas. Separation means that your delts must jut out at the side of your shoulders and "cut" sharply into the upper arms. Separation means that your serratus magnus and intercostal muscles should stand out from the side torso areas in bold relief. Separation means the abdominals should show not just in the upper reaches but in the lower area as well. Separation is the splitting of the biceps, the division of the gastrocnemeus and the appearance of the entire trapezius muscle in the middle of the back. It is the Christmas-tree effect in the lower back and the division between the two heads of the leg biceps of the back of the thigh. Separation is head-to-toe muscles that could be mistaken for a den of serpents.

DEFINITION

The lower your percentage of body fat the greater will be the appearance of your physique. This, ironically, could be dangerous if you starved yourself to the extent that you had virtually no body fat in your body at all because fat is needed in certain places to cushion the organs such as the heart, liver and kidneys. The lowest body fat I've ever heard of was around 2 percent claimed by Clarence Bass, but it's generally conceded that bodybuilders in winning condition have body fat levels of around 6 percent. Paper-thin skin that comes with this low percentage will enhance any muscle and make it look much bigger than those who don't have the same low body fat percentage. It goes without saying that if you have a very thin skin, (little or no fat) your muscles will show up to a great degree. Cross-striations of the triceps and thighs are a result of improved definition. Of course, you have to bear in mind that even the thinnest skin cannot reveal muscles or cross-striations that have not been built there in the first place. Vascularity (the appearance of veins) often goes hand in hand with definition, but it is a phenomenon of its own. Many people have definition without vascularity and, ironically, there are those who have used a lot of drugs who have incredible vascularity yet fail to show impressiveness in muscle separation. These people don't tend to do well in bodybuilding contests because the judges do not lay a great importance on vascularity unless it is accompanied by definition and muscular separation.

SHAPE AND LINE

To a great extent, the shape of your body and muscles is determined by your genes. Of course, you can improve shape by working various isolation movements to enhance this or that area. Line itself can be improved by balancing our efforts between working the various muscle groups. However, what we can do in the gym is often quite minimal as compared to what nature hands us in the first place. Genetically a poorly shaped physique with unattractive muscle insertions, narrow shoulders, large hips, and big knees cannot be totally transformed by working on the problems in the gymnasium. On the other hand, a physique that has only moderately good shape can be improved dramatically. Of course, the best of all are those who have superb shape to begin with and then go on to further enhance it by correct shape training methods. The most unfortunate instances are when a person has good natural line and shape but trains in an unbalanced fashion, and after years of bad training habits actually turns a beautiful, natural physique into an absurd shapeless mass.

To me one of the most essential aspects of bodybuilding is to train only on those exercises that enhance your overall shapeliness.

Lee LaBrada.

ARTISTRY AND DRAMA

When you pose, you need to *interest* your audience and judges. Whether you do this with slow, deliberate posing, dynamic, fast sweeping motions, or whether you choose to change the pace of your routine midway and adopt a mix of classical, brutal, balletlike, Herculean, charis-

Ed Corney.

matic or awesome poses . . . it's up to you. The free-posing section of a bodybuilding contest is your chance to show what you can do. Some bodybuilders such as Bob Paris try and tell a story with their posing. Tonya Knight is a champion of this type of presentation. Others, especially amateurs, simply go from one pose to another trying to look as big as possible. Typically, they will start with a double biceps, move into a lat spread, perform a side-chest, then go into a most muscular, and then look for ways to repeat variations of these poses. This is totally uninspiring. A true bodybuilder often feels that he or she would like to go onstage and just perform six or seven basic poses, "blow the competition away" and simply walk offstage to huge applause and win the contest outright. This never happens.

Years ago Sergio Oliva managed to pull it off because he had a very short routine and his physique was so impressive during the late 60's that he could actually pull off this type of simplistic posing and still win a contest. Today, no one can do that because they are just not far enough ahead of the competition to be able to do it. There is always somebody who can capture the judges' eyes by giving very, very impressive posing routines. I remember Ed Corney with a far less impressive physique than Frank Zane, almost taking the entire Olympia because of his amazing posing routine which trounced everybody else's and made them look like amateurs. Others followed with less than perfect bodies, but gained enormous points by championship physique display.

Today, we find bodybuilders posing to all types of music from hard rock to vocalists of all calibres. Frank Zane used to prefer Pink Floyd; Reg Park, as I said earlier, spent a dozen years posing to "Legend of the Glass Mountain." One of Arnold Schwarzenegger's favorites was "Exodus."

Posing done properly should mask the flaws in your physique, and believe me, everyone has flaws in his or her physique. There is no physique, either on the pro or the amateur circuit, that anywhere near approaches perfection. Everybody can improve. Every physique that I've ever seen has major flaws. Nobody has a perfectly proportioned physique. Even the most natural of men and women have numerous natural bodybuilding faults, some of which can be changed and some of which cannot be changed.

Arnold Schwarzenegger himself, known for being the world's best built man during the 70's would be the first to admit that his physique has inherent faults which he can only help to disguise on stage or on film rather than eliminate entirely. For example, his thighs are never really cut up, the lower parts of the thighs are certainly underdeveloped, his calves are knotty and not aesthetically shaped. They're too high. One thigh biceps has a lump in it, and his triceps are just not in line with his enormous biceps development.

Additionally, his pecs are too low and his shoulders too narrow. But in spite of all this, there's little doubt that Arnold continues to be one of the most amazing physical specimens the earth has ever known. He has an amazing ability to show himself to advantage whether clothed or unclothed. In fact, people are talking now about his charisma being so strong that even walking into a room he starts a buzz. People who have their back to him turn round sensing that somebody, almost superhuman, has walked into the room. This is a result of Arnold's natural charisma and his practice of projecting positive vibrations.

During his last Mr. Olympia contest, which was held in Australia, Arnold had not managed to train for more than five or six weeks before the event, but he had nevertheless decided that he would have one more shot at the Olympia. About halfway through the judging he realized that his physique was not as good as it could have been, and after talking to Joe Gold who said that he felt that Arnold was definitely in the top three, Arnold pulled out all the stops and almost literally forced the judges to make him a Mr. Olympia that day. He turned on his charisma and gave out such positive body language that the judges could hardly look at any other athlete onstage that day. Arnold Schwarzenegger was awarded the title over people like Chris Dickerson, Frank Zane, Boyer Coe and Mike Mentzer. Arnold later admitted that projecting himself during the judging rounds was the hardest thing he ever had to do. You can't help admiring the guy.

How do we improve our posing? Well, we start with a full-length mirror in our bedroom or bathroom, and we practice. If need be, set an overhead light a few feet in front of you to help give the impression of stage lighting, but basically work with poses that suit your particular body type. Don't be frightened to try new stances even if at first they may not seem to work totally. There is no doubt that a poor pose can become a good pose with lots of practice. At one time, Frank Zane dreaded the lat spread. He just didn't look right performing it and lost contests because it wasn't one of his better poses. In the mid-70's, however, he decided he would master the lat spread and practiced it ceaselessly. The result: It became one of his superposes, in which he could compete with any other bodybuilder in the world.

Renel Janvier.

Diana Dennis.

Regular posing will help make your individual posing routine more impressive. Posing will sharpen your upper thigh rods, add striations into the lower thighs and triceps, sharpen your serratus, and increase the delineation in the back. Posing brings out muscular detail. This is especially true in the case of the pectorals. When they are constantly flexed they develop a split and striated appearance that a person who does not pose regularly cannot duplicate. Samir Bannout is known for his constant posing. In fact, there is a joke among the pros that Samir will drop his pants at the drop of a hat, even it he's in a grocery store, to show off his thigh development. It is true that Samir is one of bodybuilding's keenest advocates and since he always feels he's in his best shape, he will show his fans or friends his muscles at *any* time, night or day. Many people conclude that Samir's amazing year-round condition is a result of his constant posing in this manner.

Who are today's top posers? Canada's Negrita Jayde has to be one of the most splendid posers of the 90's. She tells a story with her posing, lip syncs and challenges our sense of humor to give a sparkling display of stage charisma. Lee Labrada is another who keeps to posing rather than trying to tell a story, but whose positions are so tight and perfectly constructed, that he must be considered one of the world's best physique display artists. Labrada hits each pose with a flourish and holds it in such a perfect way that he invariably wins the posing round at any contest he enters. Tony Pearson is a very original poser. When he raises his shoulders and uses his unique transitions to flow from one pose to another, one gets the feeling of his being born again. Tony is a very interesting person to watch while going through his routine. Tonya Knight is another poser who totally entertains an audience with her display, and things are helped along by the fact that she is invariably in very good shape, and, of course, she has the facial and hair features of a very attractive woman, and consequently, this adds to the overall package.

Another person with an attractive face and overall body shape is Bob Paris. His posing is

Phil Hill, one of the world's best posers.

unlike any other bodybuilder's in that he will take chances with his posing and performs unconventional moves that sometimes almost shock the judges because of their originality, but nevertheless Bob Paris must be noted as one of bodybuilding's best posers.

Canadian Steve Brisbois has a certain stage charisma that puts him in the top 10 posers of the present time. Steve poses in a manner similar to Mohamed Makkawy but he also has the added ingredient of being able to move quickly in some dance-like rhythms, if he feels that a change of pace is needed.

Sometimes one feels that posing doesn't gain the points that it should in bodybuilding competition. For example, quite often the best posers do not win the posing round. This often goes to the best built person who won the previous rounds, and even though this person may not be a good poser, the judges feel that he or she should still be placed at the top of the posing round simply by merit of physical structure and muscular development. On the other hand, I have seen many a turnaround situation whereby a person who was not rated highly during the compulsory rounds then gave such a splendid performance in the free-posing and the posedown that the contest was ultimately won.

Shawn Ray of California.

CHAPTER 18 THE DAY OF THE SHOW

It could be argued that bodybuilding competition is not won during the show itself, but in the preparation during the months before a show. However, there are some do's and don'ts with regard to being the best you can be on the day of the show you are entering. It's a good idea to take more than one pair of pose trunks because oil can get on the trunks and make them rather unsightly. Having a spare makes sense.

It is also advisable to take a towel, at least two copies of your tape (the music you pose to), your oil, some tanning lotion so that if you find your color is running prior to going onstage you can touch it up, and a comb to run through your hair before appearing in front of the audience. As you are required to be backstage well before the show begins, it is a good idea to take at least two meals with you to the theatre. These should consist of a plastic bag or a plastic container in which you can take some raw vegetables, some rice, or even a few slices of chicken breast. It might also be a good idea to have some potassium tablets should you find that you are feeling weak. As for liquid, take a non-carbonated mineral water such as Evian.

The food you take prior to a show should not be excessive and should, of course, never fill the stomach. It's a good idea to have small snacks every hour prior to going onstage. This will take away some of your nervousness while posing onstage, and may also eliminate excessive shaking while you're posing. It will definitely contribute towards helping you obtain a good pump.

Pumping up is the performance of low-intensity exercises using light resistance for relatively high repetitions (20 to 40 reps). It is usually best to pump up using movements you don't usually use during your workouts. Perform them in a rhythmical, up/down tempo. (The speed at which you raise a barbell or dumbbell should be mirrored exactly when the weight is lowered.) Keep an even-paced, up/down rhythm. This will maximize your pump. I do not advocate that you do excessive pumping or that you spend more than a few minutes pumping up the muscles because excessive training will only serve to flatten out your physique. The pumping moves are lateral raises, floor dips, parallel bar dips, chins, upright rows, press and strand exercises. You may also find that the bent-over towel rows, performed with a partner, give you a good arm and back pump. If you try and really pump out the shoulders or triceps because you want that added size before appearing onstage, a little is far better than a lot. For example, if you perform a few light presses-behind-neck for the shoulders and a few lateral raises, say 2 sets of 25 of each, then you're doing far more good for your appearance than if you did 10 sets of each. If you overdo the pumping of any muscle you will tend to take away the striations of that muscle, and, consequently, the area will look smaller than it would if it had not been pumped at all.

I'm always in favor of wide-grip chinning before a contest because I feel that this pulls the scapulae out. Perform 2 or 3 sets of 10 to 15 repetitions. It is important that the scapulae be pulled out so they sit well out to the side of the torso while you're being judged onstage. I'm against excessive biceps pumping because I feel that any type of curl, although it will give more roundness to the muscle, will flatten it so that the peak aspect of your presentation of the biceps will not be as dramatic as it otherwise would if no pumping had taken place. If you do pump the biceps, limit your pumping to 1 or 2 sets of 12 to 15 reps. Do not try to push blood into the biceps to bring about a *large* additional growth.

Bill Pearl, multi Mr. Universe winner, seldom pumped up before appearing onstage at a contest. He would go through his posing routine a couple of times and generally relax until called out. His philosophy: "If I don't have it now, I never will!"

On the other hand, Sergio Oliva was known to take an entire workout before going onstage. Not many bodybuilders did that but Sergio, in fact, became famous for it. The trouble was that while standing onstage ready to pose Sergio would visibly shrink right there before the audience and judges, and this was not a particularly good way to impress people. When he first appeared onstage he looked quite huge with veins and muscles bulging all over his body, but as the contest went on he would shrink down to more normal levels. Do not regard a precontest pump as a way to increase your size at the last minute.

The reason for performing some pumping exercise is to get the heart going, keep the muscles warm, and to keep the blood flowing through the muscles. To actually not pump at all will possibly affect you negatively. Without that forcing of blood through the body and that slight state of stimulation, you can feel very thin and the mind can lose concentration if you cannot feel your muscles while onstage. Actual pumping exercises before going onstage can boost your confidence because you feel thick and built! They can put you in touch mentally with your muscles and consequently you will shine more onstage if a small or moderate amount of pumping up has been indulged in.

The following are some muscle areas that will be judged during your contest:

The Lats

With a towel and a partner you can indulge in some bent-over pulling to work the lats. Alternatively, it is a good idea to perform some chins or even some rowing exercises. If there is a lat pulldown machine backstage then you could take advantage of this by performing 2 or 3 sets of 20–25 reps in the wide-grip pulldown.

Paul Garner and Bill Richardson share a laugh while pumping backstage.

The Triceps

Pump the triceps with close-grip floor dips or light dumbbell extensions, but do not overgorge them with blood because the triceps, if worked excessively, will lose that very important delineation in muscular definition which makes them stand out onstage. It is a good idea to pump them but always keep moderation in mind.

The Pecs

The pecs traditionally have been a pumping muscle; however, most people have little trouble with their pecs and do not need to excessively pump them up or gorge them with blood. Perform a few dips on a parallel bar stand or between boxes in the backstage area. Flying exercises could be utilized as long as the weights are not too heavy.

Thighs and Calves

You may want to do a few free-standing squats to get the blood flowing in your legs or a few standing calf raises; however, avoid any type of excessive exercise in the leg area. You cannot really add much size to your calves by pumping, and you may cause a cramp that will trip you onstage, especially in the calf and thigh areas which do not respond very well to pumping exercises. If you pump up prior to your contest the deep cuts and serration between the various parts of the thigh will be lost. Pump your legs only moderately. This goes also for the thigh biceps. You cannot add size to a thigh biceps by pumping before going onstage.

Deltoids

In my opinion, the deltoids are definitely worth pumping, because the added size will give you a little more width and there will be a noticeable difference onstage if your deltoids are somewhat pumped. Try 2 to 3 sets of 15 to 20 repetitions in the press-behind-neck and a couple of sets of 15 reps in the lateral raise with dumbbells. Remember, moderation is the key. Excessive deltoid training will rob you of the separation which shows each individual head when the deltoids are viewed from the rear.

Traps

Pump this area only if it's particularly weak. Use dumbbells for shrugs and perform 2 or 3 sets of 20 repetitions. Again you will not make a great difference by pumping up your traps, but if they are particularly underdeveloped you may feel more secure if you perform a couple of sets of 20 reps.

Oiling Up

The question of how much oil to place on your body has been debated by bodybuilders for many years now. Some people swear by almond oil or walnut oil because it is believed that these actually tighten the skin, whereas a baby oil does not tighten the skin. There is no proof that almond or walnut oils do tighten the skin. The amount of oil you place on your body is important and it depends on your condition and coloring. If you have a very good tan, and you are hard and defined and have plenty of body separation, then use liberal amounts of oil. Don't be stingy. Make sure that there's oil over the entire body, the back, and the rear of the legs, and even under the arms. Do not put oil on the face. If you are inclined to be smooth, and especially if you are undertanned and white, then excessive amounts of oil will mirror the lighting situation rather than enhance your body; you will appear smooth.

Even if it's warm backstage, it's always advisable to keep your sweatsuit on until the last minute. After you have oiled yourself, if there's any time at all put the sweatsuit back on until you are ready to go onstage. At that time, remove it quickly and put a quick added coat of oil on your body, because much of the oil would have been absorbed by the sweatsuit. If you stand around backstage prior to a show and there's a draft or cool air you will find that your muscles will shrink, especially since you may have a tendency to be somewhat nervous at this stage. This will result in your muscles looking smaller and you can be sure that any vascularity you had earlier on will have vanished. Keep those muscles warm with a sweatsuit until the very last minute and you will preserve your vascularity and muscle size.

BACKSTAGE

While backstage it is a good idea to try to find an area where you can relax and mentally rehearse your routine and generally help your body unwind and prepare for the pressure that's going to come while you're onstage. Remember that being onstage during a bodybuilding contest is excessively demanding. You will have to perform not only the compulsory poses but you will also be asked to stand in such a way that the judges can view you from all angles. The likelihood is that you will be standing onstage while others are being scrutinized, but that is not to say that the judges will not be looking at you. You have to keep your thighs tensed and your abs pretty tight and your lats spread throughout the entire judging procedure.

In your effort to relax backstage don't go off in a room all by yourself unless you have someone who can come and call you when it is time to go and meet the judges and audience. More than once a competitor has missed an entire show by falling asleep or getting caught up in a backstage situation, and ultimately missed the entire contest because of lack of awareness that the contest was underway.

Always keep alert. At one Mr. Olympia (1979 Columbus, Ohio) Frank Zane, the ultimate winner, was nowhere to be found backstage. This caused some of the judging officials some confusion. In fact, he had a trailer in the parking lot where he was preparing himself, oiling and pumping up, etc., and he had somebody backstage, who, when the time was right, was to go to the parking lot and bring Zane around for the judges. Zane would turn up in his robe at pre-judging already pumped and oiled, seemingly from nowhere, and on three separate occasions he won the Mr. Olympia by following this procedure. Zane is not a great believer in psyching out the opposition. He prefers to spend the entire year in preparation for a show and ultimately turn up as near to perfection as he can be. He does not believe in involving himself in the oral games that others have become famous for.

On the other hand, Arnold Schwarzenegger proudly admits that psychological warfare is part of his game plan. On more than one occasion he has bad-mouthed bodybuilders and played a number of tricks on them to get the upper edge in the mental aspect of the competition. Even close friends are subject to ridicule onstage if it would give Big Arnold the edge. In the 1980 Mr. Olympia for example, in Australia, he claimed that his remarks to Mike Mentzer about his never becoming a Mr. Olympia because of his belly hanging out all over the stage so angered Mentzer that he couldn't pose properly during the proceedings. At other times, he supposedly walked off after a posedown and signalled Sergio Oliva to follow him suggesting that they had stayed out onstage long enough. To Oliva's detriment once he had walked offstage, Arnold quickly turned around, ran back onstage, and made gestures to Sergio to come on back and fight it out, indicating that Sergio was chicken and had refused to stay onstage and pose next to Arnold.

ONSTAGE

Once onstage it is absolutely necessary that you remain tight for the entire time that you are standing in front of those judges. When I say standing tight that means that the shoulders should be braced, the lats stretched outwards, the triceps should be hooked over the lats, the abdominals should tense, and the waist should be sucked in and kept tense. Most importantly, the thighs should be flexed so that they show their peak striations. When asked to perform the compulsory poses next to another contestant always go into the pose immediately when the head judge requests it. Do not wait for everybody else to do a double biceps and then put your own biceps up as though you're blowing them off the stage. Show your enthusiasm to compete by starting your posing immediately the judge signals which position he wants. Should you be lucky enough at the evening show to be in the top six, then you will be required to posedown with the other contestants to see who can show their muscles most advantageously. At this time it's a good idea to perform various muscular-type poses and the heavy-duty poses which show off the impressiveness of the body and limbs. The double biceps pose from the front is an example of a basic heavy-duty pose that will gain you points at this stage.

Performing artistic poses whereby the arms are stretched out and the body makes clever shapes is not advised at this stage. That should come during free-posing, which is part and parcel judged on the aesthetics of the body and posing ability. In the posedown, the judges are looking for bodybuilders to outmuscle those who are standing near them so that they can judge who is the best and most ripped physique onstage at that moment. The posedown is not a

Lee LaBrada, Lee Haney and Gary Strydom check out their triceps development.

place for the faint-hearted. You must be in condition to pose continuously, wrenching out every last drop of sweat from your body for up to five full minutes. Don't give in at this stage. Do not stop posing. Keep the movement going and work your way towards your nearest competition. Show the audience and judges that you are not frightened to pose beside the favorite of the show or the person who is nearest to challenging you for the overall title. Use one heavy-duty pose after another and do not stop any pose-down action until the judges call for an immediate cessation.

At the show's conclusion when the winners are announced if you don't place as high as you should, don't show your anger. This is no place to make a scene. It's a good lesson in sportsmanship if you grab the winner's hand and shake it and smile. Even hold it above his head. Grit your teeth and bear it. Resolve to train harder during the coming year so that next time there will be no doubt that you should be the overall winner, but for now accept the decision. There is nothing you can do about it, anyway.

History has crowned some atrocious winners in bodybuilding and, yes, some contests have been fixed in the past for one reason or another. Others appear to be fixed when in fact they are not. Generally speaking, most contests are judged as fairly as the panel of judges can carry out their task. Judging is not as easy as one might imagine because invariably judges have to balance two or more physiques where they are presented with combinations of structures so different in makeup that it is almost impossible to make a 100 percent certain assessment. For example, one bodybuilder may have large arms and no calves, and be compared to someone else who has calves but whose arms are not half as big as the first subject's. Do you penalize the man or woman who has virtually no calves, but who has enormous arms, or do you give the title to the person who has far more proportion and balance, yet who does not have exceptionally freaky large arms, like our original subject? Today in the vast majority of cases, the best man or woman wins.

It is regrettable that as a competitive bodybuilder you will often be told by your friends that you have by far the best physique in the show. This is very common among friends, who like to support their own favorites. In all my years of observing bodybuilding contests I must admit that it is extremely common for a mediocre bodybuilder to be told by friends and acquaintances when they failed to win, "You was robbed." Sometimes the advice is well meaning and the friends genuinely believe that the bodybuilder in question is superior to the rest of the competition. On the other hand, and far more likely, is the scenario whereby the bodybuilder is merely being told that he is the best onstage when in fact his so-called friends know that he should really be at the other end of the list.

Frequently, bodybuilders are not able to see how they stack up alongside their competitors even on a videotape or through the various pictures in the magazines. One finds it extremely hard to assess oneself in relation to other bodybuilders in a show. You are accompanied by 100 other people who also think they have a fantastic physique and many of these people think that they should win the show.

One final word of advice: When you're onstage do not get caught up in looking at yourself, with your head down staring at your pectorals, abdominals, or arms. This looks very amateurish to the judges and the audience alike. By all means check the light and see if you are standing in the proper light rays. Make sure they are showing up your abs and pecs but do this with a quick glance, and from that time on keep your head up looking straight out to the audience. And the winner is . . . .

Jim Quinn, a true Hercules.

INDEX

Books by
Robert Kennedy